THE CRYPTO CON

Don't Invest In What You Don't Understand.

By Andrew Brassell

Table of Contents

Copyright

Book Cover by Andrew Brassell

Illustrations by Canva.com

1st edition 2025

Dedications

"To Dione Lauter and family. You gave me a second chance at life, and I will always be eternally grateful. Thank you and God Bless you and everyone you care about. "

Sincerely, Thank you, Dionysus.

"I Think That Bitcoin At $100,000 Is The Most Ridiculous Thing.

It's not worth anything. It's the tulip bulb of our time.

It's worse than a tulip bulb because this has enabled so much criminal activity."

- Michael James Burry, American investor and hedge fund manager. Best known for predicting the subprime mortgage crisis which triggered the global financial crisis of 2008. He was portrayed in the movie The Big Short, by Hollywood actor Christian Bale.

Preface

As I sit writing this, the next great financial crisis, which will rock Western society to its core, hasn't happened yet. However, many people can feel it coming. You don't need to be an economist to sense it. The financial danger on the horizon is almost tangible—something big, something unpleasant, something so detrimental that its effects will reverberate through society for a generation is coming.

In the current prelude to this looming financial calamity, investors and financial gurus are increasingly touting the merits of cryptocurrencies like Bitcoin as supposed financial safe havens. They argue that the economic mechanics of scarcity and limited supply will see cryptocurrencies like Bitcoin boom during a major financial collapse. Some even claim that Bitcoin Jesus himself, the enigmatic Satoshi Nakamoto, created Bitcoin for this very purpose.

In many ways, cryptocurrency has evolved from obscure, hard-to-understand "nerd money" to now benefiting from an almost mythic status as a potential cure-all for the world's economic ills. However, what if Bitcoin wasn't designed to save the world from financial Armageddon? What if cryptocurrency was actually designed all along to be the eventual trigger of the next financial crisis?

At present, blind belief in Bitcoin prevents even expert blockchain and cryptocurrency developers from acknowledging glaring, fatal flaws in the basic security, viability, and economic fungibility of all forms of digital currency. There is even strong evidence to suggest that the market prices of leading cryptocurrencies like Bitcoin have been grossly and fraudulently inflated for the better part of the past decade.

None of this is to say that cryptocurrency can't make people wealthy. Millions of traders and investors have become fabulously wealthy thanks to coins like Bitcoin, and new crypto millionaires will be minted tomorrow. However, decentralized, legacy cryptocurrencies like Bitcoin will never be the money of tomorrow. As the old saying goes, it's the bank that always wins.

In The Crypto Con, I will explain in simple layman's terms why cryptocurrency cannot be trusted as a store of real wealth. I will also detail what I believe has always been the planned endgame for the current cryptocurrency market.

If you want to be the smartest person in the room when discussing the cons of cryptocurrency, keep on reading.

What Is Cryptocurrency?

In The Crypto Con, I aim to prove without reasonable doubt that all iterations of cryptocurrency currently on the market are fatally flawed from a basic cybersecurity standpoint. To do this, it is first necessary to understand what cryptocurrency is, as well as a few very basic cybersecurity concepts. To start, we will look at Bitcoin, the first-ever cryptocurrency and still the most popularly known.

The story of Bitcoin begins on the 31st of October 2008. This was the date upon which a man (though just as possibly a woman) whom we know only by the pseudonym Satoshi Nakamoto published a whitepaper titled "Bitcoin: A Peer-to-Peer Electronic Cash System" on an anonymously registered Internet domain, bitcoin.org[1].

To garner interest in his paper, Satoshi simultaneously used various communication channels to disseminate links to a full PDF copy of his whitepaper. Chief among the channels he used was a cyberpunk mailing list operated by the website metzdowd.com[2].

The exact message Nakamoto used to address subscribers to the metzdowd.com mailing list read as follows:

I've been working on a new electronic cash system that's fully peer-to-peer, with no trusted third party.

The paper is available at: http://www.bitcoin.org/bitcoin.pdf

1. http://bitcoin.org

2. http://metzdowd.com

The main properties:

- Double-spending is prevented with a peer-to-peer network.

- No mint or other trusted parties. Participants can be anonymous. New coins are made from Hashcash-style proof-of-work.

- The proof-of-work for new coin generation also powers the network to prevent double-spending.

The Bitcoin whitepaper itself reads much like an academic thesis, which must have taken Nakamoto a considerable amount of time to author. In it, he detailed the philosophical need for a new kind of ungovernable global electronic currency, while also explaining how his vision of such a currency would work.

Bitcoin itself would be a software-based transaction ledger. To more easily understand this concept, think of a bank having a list of all the names of every customer, with a separate field showing each customer's current balance. This, and a record of every other person they have ever sent money to or received money from.

In a bank, such lists/transaction ledgers exist, but they exist as private, centrally administered databases. Satoshi Nakamoto, though, wanted the Bitcoin transaction ledger to be public.

Satoshi's vision was for the Bitcoin transaction ledger to run as software called Bitcoin Core on several computers simultaneously—the more, the better. To update this ledger in any way, consensus would have to be reached among the majority of people running Bitcoin Core that any update was valid.

Let's say that Mary has some Bitcoin and she wants to send it to Tom. To do this, Mary enters into Bitcoin Core Tom's Bitcoin wallet address (the equivalent of Tom's name or account number on a regular bank transaction ledger); she then enters the amount of Bitcoin she wants to transfer from her address to Tom's and presses send. As she does this, every computer in the world running Bitcoin Core will see how much Bitcoin Mary wants to send and who to.

When everyone running Bitcoin Core agrees on the amount of Bitcoin to move and the addresses of the sender and receiver, the Bitcoin transaction ledger will be updated accordingly. What would happen, though, if someone using Bitcoin Core wanted to say that a transaction wasn't valid and instead attempted to divert Mary's Bitcoin to their own address?

To ensure that this could never happen, Satoshi Nakamoto decided to reward anyone helping process transactions with, you guessed it, Bitcoin.

When transactions are sent across the Bitcoin network, they are bundled into 2-megabyte blocks of encrypted code. Anyone running Bitcoin Core can subsequently choose to allocate some of their computer resources to help break the encryption of these blocks. This is what is referred to as Bitcoin mining.

Every time Bitcoin miners successfully break the encryption of a new transaction block, they must all reach a consensus that the transactions therein are valid. They do this by checking the existing balance of wallets sending funds and the validity of any address where Bitcoin is being sent to. In return, Bitcoin miners are rewarded with newly unlocked Bitcoin deposited to their own addresses.

Conversely, if somebody helps break the encryption of a transaction block but attempts to invalidate or alter a transaction (thereby going against the consensus reached by other miners), they receive no reward.

The Basic Economic Mechanics of Bitcoin

Thanks to the way real computational power is necessary to mine Bitcoin, Satoshi made it highly unlikely that anyone participating in the processing of Bitcoin transactions would attempt to undermine the integrity of the Bitcoin transaction ledger. After all, running a computer means spending real money on the computer itself, real money on electricity, and real money on Internet access. Why spend all of that money only to get no reward? There is just one question. Namely, how does the Bitcoin which miners are rewarded have any value?

In the real world, basic economics is driven predominantly by scarcity. Sand is commonplace and therefore has little value. However, gold and oil are scarce and become increasingly scarcer as we exhaust supplies. Because of this, we appreciate gold and oil as having more value.

Satoshi Nakamoto attempted to mirror the basic economics of scarcity in Bitcoin by encoding into Bitcoin a fixed supply of 21 million individual Bitcoins. This means that only 21 million Bitcoin will ever enter circulation. As well as this, Satoshi designed Bitcoin's core software in such a way that as more people mine Bitcoin, more computational power is required to do so. To increase scarcity further, Bitcoin is also designed in such a way that every four years, the amount of Bitcoin which miners receive as rewards for mining is reduced by 50%.

Fundamentally, of course, people still have to believe that Bitcoin has value for it to really have value. As it was, Bitcoin was going to be a hard sell to the average person on the street in 2008. This was why Satoshi

Nakamoto initially attempted to engage directly with the cyberpunks of the day.

These weren't regular people. These were ultra-nerds, programming geniuses, and veteran cryptography specialists.

These were people who got laid in Second Life and who saw infinite transformative possibilities in code and information technology. These were people, in short, who might not just understand what Satoshi Nakamoto was conceptualizing, but who might also be eager to help put his ideas to the test.

Quickly, cyberpunks ranging from Icelandic teenage programming prodigies to world-respected cryptographers began finding their way to bitcoin.org, an online forum which Satoshi Nakamoto had created especially for this purpose.

In forum posts and private messages, Satoshi Nakamoto and his growing cyberpunk community began dissecting and amending the code which would eventually become Bitcoin. Satoshi, after all, hadn't just authored a paper detailing how his vision for Bitcoin might work. Single-handedly, Satoshi had already written the entire Bitcoin codebase himself. The code also worked, arguably even better than it does today.

Today, it can take several minutes to several hours for a Bitcoin transaction to process. This is because of the ridiculously small size of Bitcoin's 2-megabyte transaction blocks. However, in the beginning, Bitcoin transacted instantly and without any transaction fees. A 2-megabyte limit on the size of transaction blocks was only added after some forum users pointed out how malicious parties might attempt to disrupt Bitcoin by intentionally flooding the early Bitcoin network with the equivalent of Bitcoin transaction spam. The goal was always to increase block sizes as more people began using Bitcoin. However, only

Satoshi could change this parameter in his code, and as we know now, Satoshi would soon disappear.

Just three months after publishing the Bitcoin whitepaper and establishing the fledgling Bitcoin community, Satoshi Nakamoto began mining the Bitcoin genesis block. This was to be the first-ever block on the Bitcoin network, one which every other transaction block would build on to create a chain of transactions. Hence, we have the term blockchain.

As Satoshi was the only user of Bitcoin at this point, the blocks which he mined were just blocks of encrypted code which released a 50-Bitcoin reward whenever their encryption was broken. There were no transactions inside which he needed to verify. However, Satoshi was aware that many people might consider Bitcoin a Ponzi scheme or self-made get-rich scheme if he retained any of the Bitcoin allocated to himself after mining the first blocks.

To this day, the first 50 Bitcoins created as Satoshi mined the Bitcoin genesis block remain locked in a Bitcoin address which even Satoshi can never access. The remainder of the 100,000 to 1 million Bitcoin which Satoshi is estimated to have mined also remains untouched.

With Bitcoin finally released into the wild as a program which anyone could download for free, several of the cyberpunks at bitcoin.org also began mining Bitcoin. They also began sending Bitcoin to each other to prove that the system worked. As they did so, Bitcoin gained a nominal value of a few fractions of a cent. After all, the very fact that people were using real computational power to swap a few bits of Satoshi's new digital money meant that at least a few people believed in it.

Eventually, the bitcoin.org community created a Bitcoin newsletter to explain and promote Bitcoin to a wider audience. They also established the world's very first Bitcoin exchange. This made it possible for people to acquire Bitcoin without participating directly in the Bitcoin network or community if they didn't want to.

Steadily, the expansion of the Bitcoin community and the improved accessibility of Bitcoin saw the cryptocurrency gain further value. Bitcoin's growth also quickly became parabolic, with prices per coin rising from mere fractions of a cent to $0.05 by mid-2010. This was thanks to people on the fringes of the cyberpunk scene realizing that whether they believed in it or not, there was demand for Bitcoin. This being the case, why not mine some?

While not a get-rich scheme, Bitcoin mining was profitable, as well as free of the risks associated with investing in or trading the digital currency.

Whether the Bitcoin price was rising or falling, people and exchanges were always willing to buy Bitcoin. At the time, mining could also be done on any mid-range home or gaming PC. With the tech required already in hand, people all around the world subsequently began mining Bitcoin, even if some weren't sure what Bitcoin actually was.

Today, things are a little different. The difficulty associated with breaking the encryption of Bitcoin transaction blocks has reached a point where specialized banks of CPUs and bleeding-edge graphics cards are required to run 24/7, just to earn a fraction of a Bitcoin. However, this is how Bitcoin began, and cryptocurrency in general is largely still based on the fundamentals which Satoshi Nakamoto outlined in his original whitepaper.

Today, the vast majority of cryptocurrencies on the market are still based on the decentralized distributed ledger technology pioneered by Satoshi Nakamoto. In fact, many coins—even Elon Musk's favorite digital currency, Dogecoin—are just clones of the original Bitcoin codebase.

How Are Other Cryptocurrencies Different from Bitcoin?

When Satoshi Nakamoto created Bitcoin, he took several precautions to ensure that Bitcoin could never be controlled by any one single entity. The whole point of Bitcoin was to be trustless and completely decentralized. Satoshi Nakamoto, therefore, released the Bitcoin codebase with an MIT General Public License. This means that Bitcoin's code is open-source and free for anyone to check for bugs, copy, and even use to create their very own cryptocurrencies.

The simplest way to create a cryptocurrency, even today, is to simply clone the software which makes up Bitcoin Core. When mining the first genesis block, new cryptocurrency developers can then change certain parameters like transaction block sizes to make their digital currency different from Bitcoin. Litecoin, one of the very first alternative cryptocurrencies to Bitcoin, did this by increasing the maximum supply of Litecoin available to mine, as well as making mining easier. Coins like Dogecoin and Dash did the same.

There are also coins today like Ethereum which have taken the Bitcoin codebase but expanded and innovated on Satoshi Nakamoto's code and ideas to create cryptocurrencies which are wildly different from Bitcoin. Ethereum, as one example, allows users to build entirely new cryptocurrencies, decentralized applications, and even web-based cryptocurrency exchanges inside of its own blockchain based virtual computer. However, this is where things start to get complicated.

Today, there are cryptocurrencies on the market like Cardano which claim to be quantum-computing resistant (this meaning that they can withstand attacks by as-yet theoretical mass-produced quantum computers). There are also coins like Monero, which claim to keep their users completely anonymous. There are also stablecoins which make it easier to trade other cryptocurrencies by always being backed on a one-to-one basis by real-world currencies like the U.S. dollar.

To detail the differences between what are now over 20,000 different cryptocurrencies currently on the market would take an entire cryptocurrency encyclopedia. The point here is to explain the basic fundamentals regarding how most cryptocurrencies work. This, and to stress that all cryptocurrencies are just software.

That cryptocurrencies like Bitcoin exist as software will be important in the remainder of The Crypto Con. This is especially true when we think of things like specialized devices like hardware wallets which some people use to store cryptocurrency.

Having a hardware wallet in your pocket or in a safety deposit box inclines people to think of cryptocurrency as something tangible stored in something secure, kept separate from exposure to threats online. The same is true when we think of cryptocurrency exchanges like Coinbase which offer to hold customer funds in so-called offline cold vaults. However, in reality, nothing could be further from the truth.

When people store cryptocurrency like Bitcoin on a physical hardware wallet or in a cold storage vault somewhere, all they do is store a cryptographic private key which represents a Bitcoin balance on the Bitcoin transaction ledger. Nothing physical exists anywhere.

Should the Bitcoin transaction ledger ever be compromised, coins held on the likes of hardware wallets will still be vulnerable to being stolen. Hardware wallets, phones, and personal computers are all also vulnerable to a wide range of cybersecurity threats, some of which are so obvious that few—especially in the cryptocurrency sphere—ever dare mention their existence.

Operation Optic Nerve

In The Crypto Con, I aim to prove that easily verifiable cybersecurity threats pose an existential threat to every form of cryptocurrency currently on the market. I will also be so bold as to suggest that these threats form part of an elaborate state-sponsored surveillance network which agencies like the U.S. National Security Agency have been busy building since at least 2008.

Sadly, mere mention of such networks is often dismissed by the average person as mere conspiracy. Since the start of the millennium, Western governments have also been extraordinarily successful in conditioning populaces that if they have nothing to hide, they have nothing to fear from such surveillance. Western society subsequently suffers from a comfortable kind of collective cognitive dissonance.

This is a sense which sees society collectively assume that only the likes of terrorists and sexual predators have anything to worry about when it comes to things like government monitoring of citizen telecommunications. Sadly, though, nothing could be further from the truth.

Remember That Time the UK Government Hacked Yahoo! To Watch You Masturbate?

No, this isn't a plot from a parody of a bad James Bond movie. This really did happen. If you grew up in the so-called naughties, MI5 (the United Kingdom's secret services) and the NSA (their North American counterparts) might still even have a few screenshots of you spanking the monkey.

As can be easily verified by Wikipedia:

- "Operation Optic Nerve is a mass surveillance programme run by the British signals intelligence agency Government Communications Headquarters (GCHQ), with help from the US National Security Agency, that surreptitiously collects private webcam still images from users while they are using a Yahoo! webcam application.

- In one 6-month period, the programme is reported to have collected images from 1.8 million Yahoo! user accounts globally. The programme was first reported on in the media in February 2014, from documents leaked by the former National Security Agency contractor Edward Snowden, but dates back to a prototype started in 2008, and was still active in at least 2012."

That's right. This isn't a matter of conjecture or so-called conspiracy theory. From 2008 until at least 2012, sophisticated wiretaps on undersea transatlantic cables were used by UK and U.S. intelligence services to record live video feeds from users of the then-popular Yahoo! Instant Messenger PC application. More specifically, screenshots of individual video conversations were taken every five minutes, and as the UK Guardian newspaper has since reported, at least 11% of all such screenshots have been confirmed to be pornographic in nature.

Sadly, this isn't the worst part. You see, Operation Optic Nerve didn't have a specific human target. It didn't even have a basic demographic target. Neither could the NSA or their British counterparts at GCHQ know before intercepting data from Yahoo-connected webcams whether the individuals subsequently being recorded were adults or minors.

What the UK government is on record as doing instead, is using early facial recognition technology to attempt to link the identities of individuals being recorded to the real-world identities of individuals held in government passport and driving license databases.

What is perhaps even more alarming about Operation Optic Nerve is that leaked NSA documents reveal that there was an aim to eventually also start tapping data from Xbox 360 and Xbox One Kinect cameras in the same way data was being harvested from Yahoo! webcams.

That's right. There really does seem to have been an active interest in targeting platforms predominantly used by children and adolescents. Neither is there any proof that Operation Optic Nerve was ever terminated. In fact, it could be argued that the UK government's 2025 implementation of mandatory identity verification of visitors to contemporary pornography websites is just Optic Nerve rebranded. After all, the UK government still ends up with a searchable database of who is masturbating to what online—even if they try to brand such ID verification as safeguarding children. (Which they certainly weren't doing in 2008.)

Your Government Likes to Have Dirt on You

If you are reading this and can reconcile yourself with the fact that Operation Optic Nerve really did happen (which it did), you are probably left wondering what the hell the whole point was. Why go to such extraordinary lengths to indiscriminately record predominantly young people in the naughties chatting and, in 11% of cases, exposing themselves on Yahoo! Messenger? In reality, though, the whole point was simple. Operation Optic Nerve was just an information-age honey trap.

To demonstrate, in May 2025, Sweden's new National Security Advisor, Tobias Thyberg, was made to stand down immediately after taking office. The reason? On hearing of his appointment, an anonymous source immediately contacted the Swedish government with illicit images of Thyberg taken while Thyberg was once chatting privately on the gay dating app Grindr.

Did a random member of the public really suddenly decide to reveal that they had illicit images of Thyberg which made him unsuited for such a position? Or was this just Optic Nerve or a Swedish program like Optic Nerve ensuring that only the right people ever occupy positions of power?

Such assumptions might sound like conspiracy theory. However, the simple fact is that state surveillance has historically been used as a tool primarily for blackmail. This has been true since at least J. Edgar Hoover's directorship of the FBI.

As the Encyclopædia Britannica states clearly:

- "Hoover habitually used the FBI's enormous surveillance and information-gathering powers to collect damaging information on politicians throughout the country, and he kept the most scurrilous data under his own personal control. He used his possession of these secret files to maintain himself as the FBI's director and was apparently able to intimidate even sitting presidents by threatening to leak damaging disclosures about them."

It is now known that Hoover himself once even went so low as to send an anonymous letter to Martin Luther King Jr., encouraging King to commit suicide rather than suffer the public exposure of several alleged affairs.

The problem today with operations like Optic Nerve and age verification checks being put in place to prevent minors from accessing pornography and even politically sensitive YouTube content, is that we subsequently live in a new kind of sex tape era. This is one in which everybody is watched and one in which everyone has something to hide. After all, who in their thirties or forties today wasn't once a teenager in the naughties keeping one eye on the bedroom door and the other on a Windows XP screen, watching something that wasn't exactly family friendly?

There is just one question: Namely, what on earth has Operation Optic Nerve and state surveillance got to do with cryptocurrency?

Hardware and Software-Based Cybersecurity Attack Surfaces

The home/personal computer revolution can be argued to have begun in 1995. Computers had been part of our lives for several decades already. However, in 1995, Jennifer Aniston and Matthew Perry from the wildly popular TV sitcom Friends were part of one of the most successful marketing campaigns in living history. Namely, that of Windows 95.

The launch of Windows 95 was when Windows first gave us the Start menu-based graphical Windows operating system metaphor, which overnight made computers easier to use for the average person than they had ever been previously. Moreover, the invention of what is still today's most popular operating system metaphor rebranded computers as must-have everything machines for any respectable home.

Any Western home which could afford one bought one. However, when anyone did, they often found themselves being simultaneously hard-sold several supposedly necessary software applications. Second on the list after Microsoft Office was usually some kind of antivirus program. This was because even the best computers could get viruses. These being wicked pieces of rogue software which could debilitate even the best machines if a respectable antivirus wasn't installed right from day one.

The hard sell is easy to see today. After all, most of the home computers being sold in 1995 weren't even being connected to the Internet. Windows 95 didn't even come bundled with its own web browser. This is not to say that antivirus programs don't play a key role in contemporary cybersecurity. The point here is to demonstrate that from the beginning of the home/personal computer revolution, users of such computers were conditioned to believe that cybersecurity threats are always software-based.

Even today, we worry about malware, trojans, and so-called zero-day exploits in the software we use to live our virtual lives through. What few people ever consider is the existence of a parallel world of much more dangerous hardware-based threats.

To make this simple to understand, Operation Optic Nerve saw the British GCHQ and American NSA physically tap undersea cables transmitting Internet data between the UK and United States. You might have had the most state-of-the-art antivirus at the time. However, there would have been no way for it to detect traffic from your computer being physically intercepted. Neither would it be possible to detect such data harvesting today.

Thankfully, even submarines or drones being used to intercept Internet data at the bottom of the ocean don't pose a threat to cryptocurrency. As discussed in the previous chapter, cryptocurrencies are never really stored or sent anywhere. There is just a transaction ledger which is amended to show changes in user balances as transactions are sent and received between different addresses. All transaction data is also encrypted, and transactions only settle when there is consensus among everyone helping process transactions that transaction details are correct.

In short, it is very easy to intercept data being sent across the likes of the Bitcoin network. However, interception isn't intervention. A malicious actor could inject malware into the likes of regular emails and software downloads when intercepting Internet traffic. However, encryption, decentralization, and mass consensus being required before any update is written into code make Bitcoin and most other cryptocurrencies immune to such attack vectors.

There is just one problem. This being that hardware taps on the likes of undersea cables and cell phone towers are just one of many tools in the average intelligence agency armory.

Does WikiLeaks Prove That the NSA Created Cryptocurrency?

In The Crypto Con, I will strive to prove that every form of cryptocurrency currently on the market has a very simple-to-understand, yet cataclysmic, vulnerability. I will also suggest that this vulnerability forms part of an elaborate signals intelligence operation implemented by the NSA.

I will now present circumstantial evidence in this chapter that Bitcoin itself may have been created by the very same U.S. National Security Agency. Specifically, as part of a long-term psychological operation to condition the general public to be accepting of purely digital payment methods that will one day supersede physical cash completely. To present this evidence, though, we must first travel back in time to 2010.

2010 was one of the most turbulent years in history for the U.S. military-industrial complex. This is at least the case when we are talking from a public relations perspective.

The PR thorn in the U.S. military and security services' side? A niche Icelandic website called WikiLeaks.

First established in 2006 by the cyberpunk-come investigative journalist Julian Assange, the Iceland-based website had become world-famous for being the place to go if you were someone wishing to leak sensitive dirt on anyone from world governments to major corporations.

Up until 2010, WikiLeaks usually hit headlines just once or twice a year. Sensitive leaks were also relatively tame in comparison to scandals that hit headlines today.

Today we have scandals like the infamous Epstein files and allegations of past and present presidents engaging in less than befitting behavior on Epstein Island. By comparison, back in the boring news days of 2008 and 2009, WikiLeaks mic drops often equated to just leaked 9/11 pager messages and a few embarrassing emails sent by Sarah Palin. However, in 2010, WikiLeaks really started to kick the hornet's nest.

Starting with a video of an American Apache helicopter firing on civilians and Reuters journalists in Iraq, WikiLeaks in 2010 began dropping truth bomb after truth bomb. In July, WikiLeaks published the now infamous Afghan War Logs. This was followed by an October release of the now just as infamous Iraq War Logs. These totaled what amounted to over 475,000 pages of highly classified military and security services documents—and the U.S. was pissed.

The last quarter of 2010 subsequently saw arrest warrants issued for WikiLeaks founder Julian Assange, then a manhunt for Assange, with all of this accumulating in Assange eventually seeking political asylum in the official embassy of Ecuador in London. There he would stay until 2019 to prevent being extradited to the United States. Meanwhile, other WikiLeaks associates like Arjen Kamphuis, a leading Dutch cybersecurity expert, were slowly hunted down and disappeared up until as recently as 2018.

Going back to 2010, with the U.S. thwarted from getting its man and cutting the head off the WikiLeaks snake, U.S. officials quickly implemented a new WikiLeaks silencing strategy. If they couldn't incarcerate those involved with WikiLeaks, they would simply starve WikiLeaks to death financially. As this strategy was implemented, the mainstream media narrative surrounding WikiLeaks flipped instantly.

Where previously newspapers and news anchors on television had recoiled in horror at WikiLeaks' leaked slayings of innocent civilians and journalists, the mainstream media narrative shifted its focus entirely onto the supposed danger that such leaks were posing to military personnel still active in Iraq and Afghanistan. Now, WikiLeaks was the enemy.

As this narrative was reaffirmed over and over by news anchor after news anchor, the U.S. government began pressuring payment services like Visa, Mastercard, Maestro, Amex, and PayPal to drop all support for WikiLeaks. This they did, completely starving WikiLeaks of donations and effectively debanking the organization in one fatal financial swoop.

Enter Bitcoin

If anyone googles the creation of Bitcoin, they will today stumble upon several news articles hailing Bitcoin as a revolutionary form of currency. A currency born out of the angst of the 2008 financial crisis. However, in truth, Bitcoin didn't receive a single mainstream media mention at all until late 2010, over two years after Satoshi Nakamoto first published the original Bitcoin whitepaper.

Between 2008 and 2010, Bitcoin was a ghost in the internet machine. No one on Earth aside from the people whom Satoshi Nakamoto had invited to his Bitcoin.org forum and a few of their nerdy friends knew that Bitcoin even existed. In fact, there are literally no mentions of Bitcoin at all on social media, Google, the mainstream media, or anywhere else until over a year after the Bitcoin genesis block had been mined.

Bitcoin was essentially a big nerdy secret being kept among a few hundred people from the original Bitcoin mailing list, but not everyone was happy about this.

Seeing WikiLeaks, which itself was a cyberpunk movement, be dealt death blow after death blow by the U.S. government, some in Satoshi

Nakamoto's fledgling Bitcoin community were eager to use Bitcoin to offer support.

One poster on the Bitcoin.org forum known only as RHorning wrote directly to Satoshi Nakamoto on December 4th, 2010 to say:

- "Basically, bring it on. Let's encourage WikiLeaks to use Bitcoins and I'm willing to face any risk or fallout from that act."

In response, Satoshi Nakamoto himself replied with the following:

- "No, don't 'bring it on.' The project needs to grow gradually so the software can be strengthened along the way. I make this appeal to WikiLeaks not to try to use Bitcoin. Bitcoin is a small beta community in its infancy. You would not stand to get more than pocket change, and the heat you would bring would likely destroy us at this stage."

Despite this plea, one of Satoshi Nakamoto's crypto apostles did eventually reach out to WikiLeaks. To Nakamoto's dismay, this saw WikiLeaks begin accepting Bitcoin donations just two months later.

Now, let's take a pause to think about this logically.

At this point in time, Bitcoin existed as just a few hundred people mining the cryptocurrency and exchanging it to prove a proof of concept. Satoshi Nakamoto was, therefore, right to be worried about Bitcoin garnering too much attention too quickly.

Bitcoin could have easily been destroyed by agencies like the NSA. They could have attacked the mere handful of Bitcoin miners that there were at the time with a simple denial-of-service attack. To obliterate Bitcoin even easier, such agencies could have pressured internet service providers to cut off internet access to Bitcoin miners, or even the entire

Bitcoin community. We are talking, after all, about the very same state actors who had just pressured all the world's payment processors to de-bank WikiLeaks. Putting similar pressure on a few internet service providers would have been easy. A question must, therefore, be asked, and the question is this one:

Why, out of every single payment service in the world, did the U.S. government allow Bitcoin to be used to fund WikiLeaks, when it was the easiest, both practically and legally, to obliterate? Because this did happen. Moreover, what also happened as Bitcoin entered the mainstream media spotlight for the first time was the start of the Bitcoin Streisand Effect.

The Bitcoin Streisand Effect

For those not familiar with the concept, the so-called "Streisand effect" can best be described as reverse psychology in action. Someone tells you not to look at something, but this only results in you wanting to look harder at the subject matter in question.

The Streisand effect gets its name from a single aerial photograph of the home of the actress Barbra Streisand taken in 2003. Not happy about its publication online, Barbra Streisand attempted to sue the photographer, Kenneth Adelman, even though the photograph in question had only been viewed and downloaded from online a total of six times.

Sadly for Barbra Streisand, her lawsuit and efforts to scrub the image in question from the internet only resulted in a massive 420,000 views and downloads of the image of her home over the course of the next 30 days.

With Bitcoin, which was miraculously allowed to survive by the U.S. government, a similar Streisand effect took place. WikiLeaks, but more so WikiLeaks' new funding source, were suddenly world news. What was this new form of so-called digital currency? How had it thwarted a worldwide financial embargo on WikiLeaks? And most importantly of all, should you buy some, or was Bitcoin just air money?

The WikiLeaks narrative that had dominated headlines throughout 2010 had been flipped once again, only this time more ingeniously. First there was outrage against war crimes. Next there was outrage against the exposure of war crimes, and then suddenly, there was Bitcoin.

Bitcoin. Bitcoin. No war crimes to see here, just Bitcoin. What is Bitcoin?

At the exact time that Bitcoin began garnering real media attention—and to make this clear, any media attention at all since its genesis—Satoshi Nakamoto, its creator, also disappeared completely.

"I am moving on to other things," was Nakamoto's last ever message on Bitcoin.org. Only for mere days later the CIA to reach out to fellow Bitcoin.org forum user Gavin Andresen to request a full official briefing on what Bitcoin actually was.

Are WikiLeaks and the Silk Road Bitcoin's Smoking Gun?

When you understand how Bitcoin works, it is perplexing, to say the least, to understand how Bitcoin was allowed to survive after intervening in the battle for WikiLeaks' survival. However, what is even more perplexing is how Bitcoin was allowed to survive when, in tandem with Bitcoin becoming more widely known, it immediately became the currency of choice for users of the illicit dark web Silk Road marketplace.

Ross Ulbricht, himself a Bitcoin.org member, founded the now infamous dark web marketplace at almost exactly the same time that WikiLeaks began accepting Bitcoin donations. You can, therefore, be sure that the likes of the NSA and other intelligence agencies all quickly had Bitcoin on their radar. The founding of the Silk Road also gave these agencies all of the moral ammunition they needed to take Bitcoin down forever.

The U.S. government had used the supposed danger that continued WikiLeaks leaks posed to active military personnel to justify an unprecedented financial embargo on WikiLeaks. Now that Bitcoin was being used on the dark web to buy everything from drugs to firearms (and even more illicit materials), what more justification did the powers that be need to nip the new digital currency in the bud?

As Bitcoin was to grow as a network, it would become nearly impossible for governments or intelligence services to take down or even significantly disrupt. Such agencies must also have known this. Why then was Bitcoin still allowed to persist?

There is no direct evidence that I am aware of that proves that Bitcoin was always an intelligence agency creation. However, such agencies turning a blind eye to Bitcoin is to me something of a smoking gun. For some reason, Bitcoin seems to have been protected. Even more curiously, so too do some of the people who would go on to help the fledgling cryptocurrency become the monolith that it is today.

The Strange Case of the Silk Road & The Trial of Ross Ulbricht

Eventually, the dark web marketplace the Silk Road was taken down by the FBI. The case against its founder, Ross Ulbricht, was also apparently an open-and-shut one. Ulbricht admitted to the FBI that he had created the Silk Road, and computers seized from Ulbricht clearly showed that he had been actively administering the dark web marketplace at the time of his arrest. However, how the FBI managed to take down the Silk Road is something of an enigma.

Officially, the FBI states that CAPTCHA technology being used by the Silk Road was accidentally leaking the otherwise hidden real IP address of the marketplace. This allowed the FBI to discover the Silk Road's real-world server and admin login page. However, several cybersecurity researchers have since stated that this exploit simply didn't exist at the time. This implies that the FBI gained access to the Silk Road server and admin page via some other undisclosed means.

There are other incongruities in the case against Ulbricht. One of the most significant being that Ulbricht admitted to creating the Silk Road but also claimed that he had relinquished all control of the dark web marketplace shortly afterward. Then, just as the FBI was closing in, the Silk Road's real mastermind, one Mark Karpelès, had tricked Ulbricht into returning to the Silk Road to administer the site.

Mark Karpelès—Bitcoin's Multipurpose Man of Teflon

Mark Karpelès was not someone unknown to the cryptosphere. On the 24th of June 2011, Satoshi Nakamoto's original Bitcoin.org forum was migrated to a new BitcoinTalk.org domain hosted by Mark Karpelès. This can be confirmed by still accessible message threads on the Bitcoin forum.

- "Change of hosting

  Mark Karpelès is now hosting the forum's server. The forum is still owned by Sirius, as it has always been. There will be no policy changes."

Quote from: BitcoinTalk.org user theymos on September 11, 2011, 04:17:26 AM

Why does it matter that Mark Karpelès now hosted the original Bitcoin forum? Well, only because he was the CEO of a brand new Bitcoin exchange called Mt. Gox. This—and as revealed by FBI special agent Jared Der-Yeghiayan after he began investigating the Silk Road—the silkroadmarket.org (the hidden front end of the Silk Road) and bitcointalk.org were from September 2011 to February 2013 both hosted by a Mark Karpelès hosting company called Mutum Sigillum LLC, which also hosted Mt. Gox.

That's right. The Silk Road, Mt Gox, and Satoshi's original Bitcoin forum were all hosted for 2 years by the same Mark Karpelès hosting company, while Karpelès was himself CEO of Mt Gox.

Even more intriguing is the fact that FBI agent Jared Der-Yeghiayan was able to prove that both of the forums at silkroadmarket.org and bitcointalk.org ran the same versions of the same outdated forum software.

Now to be clear, it can be said for certain that the Karpelès-owned hosting company hosting the Silk Road, BitcoinTalk, and Mt Gox would have been able to discover the Silk Road official admin/login page that the FBI eventually used to hack its way into the site. All web hosting plastforms can do this.

This would imply that it was possibly Karpelès who gave the FBI details of the Silk Road admin page. Moreover, if he knew the FBI was closing in (which he did due to the Department of Homeland Security investigating Mt Gox and Mutum Sigillum LLC from as early as May 2013, and the Silk Road not being shut down until October), this would be the logical thing to do. All Karpelès would have to do first is secure a suitable fall guy—and who better than the person who built your dark web illicit marketplace for you in the first place?

All of this is, of course, conjecture. However, Mark Karpelès wasn't exactly of squeaky-clean character. Karpelès had already been convicted of fraud in France in absentia in 2010, investigated in France for computer crimes, and would later be found guilty in Tokyo of falsifying Mt. Gox data to inflate Mt. Gox's holdings by $33.5 million in 2014.

It would also be revealed in later investigations in Japan into the collapse of Mt. Gox that a presumed Mt. Gox insider had been siphoning Bitcoin from exchange user accounts from as early as 2011. Karpelès is also alleged to have known about this right until the collapse of the exchange in 2014. At one point, FBI agent Jared Der-Yeghiayan was also personally convinced that Karpelès was using both the Silk Road and Mt. Gox to artificially increase the price of Bitcoin to cover Mt. Gox losses.

Be that as it may, in the third week of the trial against Ross Ulbricht, something strange happened.

In January 2015, presiding Judge Katherine Forrest ruled that any speculation that Mark Karpelès was the real mastermind of the Silk Road and that Ulbricht was duped by him into becoming a fall guy for the FBI would not be admissible in any future testimony. All such statements from previous testimony would also be stricken from the existing record.

It is almost like someone or some agency was protecting Karpelès.

The Silk Road Saga Today

During his first full day of office in 2025, President Donald Trump gave Ross Ulbricht a complete presidential pardon, effectively quashing his conviction of being the mastermind behind the Silk Road. He justified this by citing FBI overreaches and the existence of too many holes in the original prosecution's case against Ulbricht.

Ross Ulbricht has since retreated into anonymity. However, Mark Karpelès continues to bask in the Bitcoin limelight.

To date, he's been founder of Tibanne, possibly the first company in the world to accept Bitcoin payments. Karpelès has also hosted Satoshi Nakamoto's original Bitcoin forum, the Silk Road, and Mt. Gox; been a founding member of the official Bitcoin Foundation; CEO of Mt. Gox; survived the collapse of Mt. Gox; bizarrely been allocated millions of dollars after the official bankruptcy of the site (despite being convicted of falsifying Mt. Gox account data)—and since gone on to found the Bitcoin exchange EllipX.

Bitcoin Was Never the Monetary Revolution You Were Made to Believe It Was

This chapter of The Crypto Con will have been a hard read. Some things that I have stated are also matters of conjecture. However, the facts that I have presented here are verifiable facts.

Bitcoin could have easily been destroyed—and justifiably so—when it simultaneously became the currency of choice for WikiLeaks and the Silk Road in early 2011. In this case, why wasn't it? How also did Satoshi Nakamoto's original Bitcoin Forum, the illicit marketplace the Silk Road, and Bitcoin's first ever mainstream exchange, Mt. Gox, all happen to become hosted at the exact same time by the same hosting company?

All of this did happen. However, when anyone investigates the Bitcoin origin story, they are presented with the fairy tale of a messiah-like individual known only by a Japanese pseudonym, who gave the world digital currency before vanishing forever into the Internet ether. Few ever mention how Bitcoin arrived in tandem with the Silk Road. Nor how Bitcoin's first innovators were all known to each other, interacted, and in some cases, were constantly dogged by allegations of financial mischief.

Neither does anyone ever mention just how easy Bitcoin would have been to destroy when it was still primarily being used as the currency of choice for illicit transactions on the dark web.

There has, if you like, been a very big blockchain brush sweeping many undesirable Bitcoin talking points under a very big cryptocurrency rug for several years. Cryptocurrency, after all, isn't something that you are really supposed to think about. You are just supposed to buy it to get rich and accept the virtuous Satoshi Nakamoto mythos.

The only question is: Just how much more dirt is there under the crypto carpet?

Bitcoin Today Is the Antithesis of the Bitcoin Satoshi Nakamoto Conceptualized

So far in The Crypto Con, I have attempted to explain in layman's terms how cryptocurrencies like Bitcoin work. I have also suggested that Bitcoin itself may have always been a deep state creation, one seeded in society to slowly condition populaces to be accepting of a one-day completely cashless future where all money is digital. (Albeit not in the same way that cryptocurrencies like Bitcoin are today.)

Whether I am right or wrong doesn't matter, for regardless of what you want to believe, one thing is certain. This being that Bitcoin today is the complete antithesis of what Satoshi Nakamoto, if he ever existed, originally envisaged his digital currency being.

The Bitcoin You Know Vs. The Bitcoin You Think You Know

To start with a few basics, Bitcoin is not peer to peer as it is often claimed. Calling Bitcoin peer to peer implies that you can send Bitcoin from a wallet you own to someone else's without any intermediary. However, unless you are actively mining Bitcoin on your computer, you will today depend on Bitcoin's network of miners to process transactions for you. You will also pay a fee ranging from a few cents to a few dollars for the privilege. Bitcoin by definition is, therefore, not peer to peer.

Now, if you use cryptocurrency, let me ask you a further question: Are you yourself actively running a Bitcoin transaction node or actively mining any form of cryptocurrency in which you are invested?

The likely answer to this question will be no. In fact, in my 10+ years working in the crypto space, I have yet to meet a single member of the public who, despite investing in digital currency, actually runs a node or mines cryptocurrency themselves. And this is a problem.

Why helping blockchains like the Bitcoin blockchain process transactions matters is simple. In the Bitcoin whitepaper, it was made clear that Satoshi Nakamoto foresaw a future in which the majority of people using Bitcoin would also be active participants in the maintenance of the Bitcoin blockchain itself.

Rather than having mining farms, which today make it impossible for individual miners to make a profit mining Bitcoin, Satoshi envisaged a future in which almost all Bitcoin users would run Bitcoin's core software on their computers. The more people who did this, the better for Bitcoin.

Decentralization Is Fundamental to Bitcoin Security

From a security standpoint, to disrupt the Bitcoin transaction network, you have to disrupt Bitcoin miners, on whom the network depends to process transactions. The more miners there are, the more difficult it is to interfere with transactions in any way. This is especially true when Bitcoin mining is distributed among millions, or as Satoshi Nakamoto originally envisaged, hundreds of millions of individual computers worldwide. At the same time, when more people actively mine Bitcoin, the more equitable Bitcoin itself becomes as a form of currency.

More people mining Bitcoin means that Bitcoin itself becomes more equitably distributed among the general population. If we had more individual Bitcoin miners today, we would subsequently have fewer so-called "Bitcoin whales" who own vast amounts of the digital currency and who, by doing so, can manipulate market prices through coordinated buying and selling.

The Reality of Bitcoin Mining and Decentralization Today

Sadly, while Bitcoin mining was initially popular during the early days of Bitcoin, the so-called CPU mining era of Bitcoin only lasted until exactly the 10th of May 2010. Until this point, it was possible for anyone anywhere to mine Bitcoin with a reasonably powerful computer. The better your CPU was—the best being Intel's Xeon X5680 six-core, 130-watt, 3.33GHz CPU—the more Bitcoin you could mine. It was also during the so-called CPU mining era from 2009 to 2010 that Bitcoin was the most decentralized that it has ever been since. Then something happened.

On the 10th of May 2010, Bitcoin community member Laszlo Hanyecz, famous for being the first person to ever buy pizza with Bitcoin, made a discovery. Laszlo found that it was possible to use the NVIDIA graphics card of his Mac computer to mine far more Bitcoin than he could with his CPU.

- "Updated Mac OS X binary...It will use your GPU to generate bitcoins. This works really well if you have a good GPU like an NVIDIA 8800 or something like that."

— ***Original message posted by Hanyecz to the Bitcoin Talk forum.***

Using graphics cards (GPUs) to mine cryptocurrency works better than using a computer's CPU, thanks to the fact that graphics cards are capable of much more powerful parallel processing. It was quickly found that it was also possible to create banks of graphics cards to mine far more Bitcoin than would ever be possible with regular CPU mining. Moreover, this was something which Satoshi Nakamoto himself never expected.

We know that the possibility of GPU mining passed under Nakamoto's radar when conceptualizing Bitcoin, as Nakamoto himself reached out to Laszlo Hanyecz directly to express concerns about where GPU mining might take Bitcoin. We also know now that Nakamoto's concerns were well founded.

Goodbye True Decentralization and True Equitability

As soon as it was discovered that it was possible to mine Bitcoin using widely available NVIDIA graphics cards, true Bitcoin decentralization began to suffer as mining started to be consolidated among those who could afford to purchase and operate the most NVIDIA GPUs simultaneously.

Bitcoin was no longer peer to peer, equitable, or decentralized to the extent Satoshi Nakamoto originally envisaged it would one day be. Instead, Bitcoin began to parallel the same flaws inherent in the existing financial paradigm. Those who could afford the most bleeding-edge graphics cards would now come to monopolize the entire fledgling Bitcoin economy.

If we fast forward in time from 2010 to the present, we now have a cryptocurrency market that bases itself on the same principles which Satoshi supposedly hated.

Every day, new cryptocurrencies and tokens are created out of thin air, which fuel rampant speculation and bring about massive pump-and-dumps. However, this is apparently okay, as all such schemes fall under the banner of what contemporary cryptocurrency proponents call "decentralized finance" (DeFi).

Bitcoin itself is now also largely institutionalized. While we still have a few independent Bitcoin whales who mined or bought their stash right at the beginning, we are now seeing large institutions like MicroStrategy and BlackRock dominate commercial supply. BlackRock's iShares Bitcoin Trust, for example, currently controls 5.9% of the total global supply of Bitcoin. So much for equitability.

Bitcoin mining is now also consolidated into ever-smaller groups. These are known as mining farms, and as well as making it impossible for independent miners to mine Bitcoin, reduced distribution of miners increases the possibility of security threats such as a 51% attack on the Bitcoin blockchain.

To demonstrate just how un-decentralized Bitcoin is at present, The New York Times revealed in 2023 that a whopping one-third of all Bitcoin mining was already consolidated among just 22 different mining entities, half of which operate out of Texas. This is a far cry from Satoshi's original vision of having mining equally distributed among anyone anywhere mining Bitcoin with a reasonably powered personal computer.

We are also at a point in time where some of the biggest players in the cryptocurrency space may be about to start exploiting the ignorance of new-to-market investors. BlackRock, for example, recently made a claim that at some point, the set total amount of Bitcoin to ever be created may be increased past the current cap of 21 million. Likewise, the cryptocurrency exchange Binance has suggested that it may one day be possible to roll back the Bitcoin blockchain to reverse Bitcoin thefts and funds sent in error to miscellaneous addresses. (Much like how current bank chargebacks work.)

If you know anything about Bitcoin, you will know that such ideas amount to Bitcoin heresy. The whole point of Bitcoin being decentralized was to prevent powerful entities from freezing or rolling back accounts, and most sacrilegious of all, ever creating new Bitcoin.

Sadly, we are at a point in time where more people than ever believe that Bitcoin and other cryptocurrencies have value. However, we are also at a point in time where few investing in Bitcoin or other cryptocurrencies know how Bitcoin works or was ever intended to work.

Bitcoin Has Less Intrinsic Value Today Than It Did in 2009

Make no mistake: If Bitcoin mining continues to consolidate among a select wealthy few, making changes to the Bitcoin blockchain will be possible.

It will be possible to increase the total Bitcoin supply. It will also be possible to roll back transactions. However, this would see Bitcoin become no different to the cash we have today.

When/if this happens, the basic premise of Bitcoin as permissionless and decentralized will be completely broken. Bitcoin will also fail to have any true intrinsic value. The basic economic mechanics of Bitcoin, after all, are based on scarcity and Bitcoin's total supply becoming scarcer over time. Bitcoin is also supposedly permissionless and immutable. This means that Bitcoin balances can never be frozen or confiscated by third parties like central banks or governments.

Some may argue that being permissionless makes Bitcoin and other cryptocurrencies ideal vehicles for tax avoidance. However, one reason why Bitcoin was designed this way was to prevent the equivalent of bank bail-ins where banks and central governments confiscate wealth to recapitalize during financial crises.

While such bail-ins might seem absurd, this is exactly what happened in Cyprus in 2013. Major banks were prevented from collapse by confiscating customer deposits. Likewise, at the start of the Great Depression in 1933, the U.S. government of Franklin D. Roosevelt used Executive Order 6102 to force U.S. citizens to sell any gold they owned to the government at a rate far below then-market prices. Not declaring gold you owned, hoarding gold, and not selling gold to what was essentially the Federal Reserve was made a criminal act under the same order.

If it were not for Bitcoin being permissionless and Bitcoin transactions being completely immutable (impossible to interfere with), it would never have been possible for Bitcoin to be used as a financial lifeline for WikiLeaks. Worse, we already have evidence that the poor true decentralization of Bitcoin today is already having a negative effect on the basic censorship resistance which first saw Bitcoin rise to power.

Bitcoin Today Is No Longer Truly Censorship Resistant

As well as scarcity, utility, and diminishing supply, the intrinsic value of Bitcoin and other cryptocurrencies often centers on the unmalleability of cryptocurrency transactions and their subsequent censorship resistance. The very idea that any third party—be it a hacker, government, or government agency—could ever prevent a Bitcoin address from sending or receiving funds is antithetical to the core principles of Bitcoin.

Sadly, diminished true decentralization today now sees Bitcoin susceptible to government interference when it comes to the basic settlement of transactions. Neither is this a matter of conjecture. Right now, third parties can put pressure on Bitcoin's miners to refuse to process transactions.

The first evidence we have of this comes from 2023, when as part of a Bitcoin mining pool observer project conducted by the Bitcoin developer B10C, it was found that one of the world's top three mining pools was actively preventing certain Bitcoin addresses from receiving funds.

To be more specific, F2Pool, the mining pool in question, was found by B10C to be applying a filter to prevent several Bitcoin transactions from ever settling. After further investigation, B10C found that all of the transactions in question could be linked to Bitcoin addresses on an official list of addresses suspected of criminality issued by the U.S. government's Office of Foreign Assets Control (OFAC).

If a Bitcoin address appears on the OFAC list, this means that U.S. authorities are attempting to apply sanctions to the person or group operating the address in question. There might also be legitimate reasons for this. However, it is important to focus on three key points here:

- Bitcoin supposedly benefits from global decentralization. The Office of Foreign Assets Control, therefore, has no way to enforce the confiscation or freezing of any Bitcoin being sent to or from any wallet.

- F2Pool operates out of Asia. F2Pool, therefore, has no legal obligation to comply with OFAC requests to freeze or interfere with any Bitcoin wallet transaction.

- Immutable transactions that are impossible to reverse or censor were once one of the key reasons Bitcoin had value. Let's remember again, for example, that WikiLeaks was the

> first major adopter of Bitcoin after WikiLeaks was blacklisted by PayPal and every other global payment processor at the behest of the U.S. government.

By F2Pool's own admission, censoring transactions going to or from OFAC addresses was easy. The pool's co-founder, Chun Wang, simply applied a transaction filtering patch to the entire F2Pool mining pool, which took hashing power away from transactions going to or from known OFAC addresses. This effectively left transactions in Bitcoin limbo.

As for why F2Pool made the decision to help the OFAC attempt to block Bitcoin transactions, we will likely never know. All we do know for certain is that this has already taken place. There is, therefore, now a precedent for mining pools working to undermine the integrity of Bitcoin. Also worth noting is the fact that at the time of writing, F2Pool, (on average), currently processes 14% of all global BTC transactions.

I'm Not a Criminal—Why Should I Worry About Whether Bitcoin Is Censorship Resistant?

As the old saying goes, "If you have nothing to hide, you have nothing to fear." Really, though, this is just government propaganda used to justify the ever-further erosion of modern society's presumed right to privacy.

Some might see Bitcoin mining pools bending to the will of law enforcement agencies as a good thing. Let us not forget, though, that just a few years ago, the Canadian government set about freezing the bank accounts of people protesting COVID-19 mandates. Likewise, as already noted with regard to WikiLeaks, let us also remember that one of the first things even supposedly democratic governments do to whistleblowers is decouple them from their finances.

The simple fact is that Bitcoin, by nature, was intended to be resistant to such state interference. Now, it isn't. This being the case, if you invest in Bitcoin today, you are not investing in anything like the original Bitcoin of 2009 which made a lot of people rich because they believed in the fundamental ideals of the cryptocurrency. You are instead just investing in the shadow of the monolith Bitcoin used to be before it was bent and twisted slowly to become just a brand with as much true financial nutritional value as your average Happy Meal.

The Unspoken Vulnerability of EVERY Cryptocurrency

So far in The Crypto Con, I have attempted to give readers a basic understanding of how cryptocurrencies like Bitcoin work. I have also attempted to make a clear distinction between software-based and hardware-based cybersecurity threats. This is due to the fact that in this chapter, I will expose a fundamental hardware flaw inherent in almost every modern personal computer, which undermines the basic security of every form of cryptocurrency. It's not a flaw, though—not really.

Before I continue, please recall Operation Optic Nerve, which I discussed at length in Chapter Two. This was a verified NSA and GCHQ surveillance operation that saw intelligence agencies intercept data from Yahoo!-connected webcams.

The 2008-to-2012 operation only came to light thanks to the NSA whistleblower Edward Snowden. This does not mean to say, though, that the same agencies then suddenly ceased such mass domestic state surveillance. Rather, the NSA's longtime cyber nemesis WikiLeaks has since proven that such surveillance has only intensified.

Operation Weeping Angel

In a series of leaks published by WikiLeaks in 2017 known as Vault 7, it was revealed that the CIA had for several years been utilizing malware embedded in the hardware of Samsung F-series smart televisions, which could remotely record images and audio from smart TV users. The malware in question was codenamed Weeping Angel.

Below is an excerpt of an actual Project Weeping Angel "Accomplishments" progress report:

Weeping Angel (Extending) Engineering Notes SECRET // REL USA,UK Accomplishments during joint workshop with MI5/BTSS (week of Jun 16, 2014)

- Discovered delete and download keyfiles are sensitive to any newline characters.
- Found configuration file and setting that manages automatic updates.
- Added feature to periodically re-acquire alsa (audio) device while in Fake-Off mode.
- Suppress LEDs to improve look of Fake-Off mode.
- Ported and modified TinyShell to provide shell, command execution, file transfer. This version is known as pshell since its shell functionality is really a wrapper around popen() calls to emulate shell-like functionality.
- Added feature to prevent updates (an iptables rule—ported iptables application to this platform).
- Received sanitized source code from UK with comms and encryption removed.

Weeping Angel is, therefore, not speculation. After WikiLeaks exposed the surveillance technique, Samsung itself was forced to start updating smart TV user guides to warn consumers not to have sensitive conversations around appliances, even when devices were powered off. This was thanks to Weeping Angel's malware being impossible for even Samsung to remove or detect in its own appliances.

Bitcoin Was Compromised Right From the Beginning

It is now that things will start to hit home a little harder.

If we go back in time to 2008 and Satoshi Nakamoto publishing the original Bitcoin whitepaper, we go back in time to an age when most of the best personal computers on the market were being shipped with dual-core processors manufactured by Intel. For gamers and businesses looking for a little more than 2.9 GHz of processing power, there was also the world's first line of multi-core processors, such as the Core 2 Quad Q6600.

For all intents and purposes, these processors were just as secure as any basic Celeron or Pentium processor before them. This means that if you were worried about cybersecurity threats in 2008, the threats you were worried about were almost always going to be software-based. Security-conscious computer users could, therefore, rest assured that local data stored on their PCs was safe, providing they were using software tools like regularly updated antivirus applications.

It is of fundamental importance to also understand that this is the cybersecurity environment in which Satoshi Nakamoto, the creator of Bitcoin, envisioned Bitcoin operating in, as well as continuing to evolve in. There is just one problem: This being that within days of Satoshi Nakamoto publishing the Bitcoin whitepaper, something that would forever change the nature of the cybersecurity landscape we live in happened.

ANDREW BRASSELL

Intel Inside or NSA Inside?

Imagine having a computer inside your computer—one that you don't even know is there. Better yet, imagine having a computer with its own operating system and networking capabilities baked right into the same CPU your current computer uses. I'm talking about a literal second computer, one which you don't know about and can't access, but one which can, whenever it wants, access all your data and files, even when your machine is powered off.

Most consumer PC and laptop users won't be able to comprehend such a machine. However, this machine exists. It is called the Intel Management Engine, and it has been baked into every Intel-manufactured CPU since 2008.

The official purpose of the Intel Management Engine (IME) is to serve as a dedicated hardware subsystem for Intel's Active Management Technology (AMT). This allows for remote, out-of-band (OOB) management of servers and computers, even when devices are powered off, and even when device operating systems are unable to boot.

In layman's terms, the out-of-band management capabilities of Intel's Management Engine allow anyone with IME subsystem access to bypass security challenges like computer administrator passwords and even full disk encryption of computer hard disks. Being able to bypass device security so completely allows the IME to access any data on devices (encrypted or not), make changes to device operating systems and firmware, and even control any connected peripherals with full administrator privileges.

The IME, if you like, is Weeping Angel on steroids.

Is the IME a Dedicated Backdoor or a Cybersecurity Oversight?

Stating that anyone with access to the Intel Management Engine will subsequently be able to take full control of host computers and easily access even ultra-secure encrypted files and databases is not a matter of conjecture.

2025.1 IPU - Intel® Chipset Firmware Advisory

Summary:

- Potential security vulnerabilities in Intel® Converged Security and Manageability Engine (CSME), Intel® Active Management Technology (AMT), and Intel® Standard Manageability firmware may allow information disclosure, denial of service, or escalation of privilege.

- Intel is releasing updates to mitigate these potential vulnerabilities.

The above is just one of several periodically issued advisory statements by Intel, highlighting newly found exploits in the IME which make possible (in Intel's own words) "information disclosure"—meaning theft of data, "escalation of privilege"—meaning control of computers and devices, and denial-of-service attacks.

Right from the beginning, when Intel began embedding the IME in CPUs, Intel could have mitigated such security exploits by making the complete codebase which the IME runs on open-source and available for independent security analysis. Instead, Intel decided to make all IME data proprietary and rely instead on the idea of security by obscurity.

Put simply, Intel still relies on the assumption that if no one knows that the IME exists, no one will attempt to use it as a security exploit. This is why even today, some of the most cybersecurity-aware computer users have no idea that the IME is likely running on their own hardware. The only question is, was the IME developed specifically to act as a backdoor in the first place?

Unlike with the likes of Operation Optic Nerve and Project Weeping Angel, it cannot be stated conclusively that the IME was developed and rolled out with purposeful intelligence agency instruction or surveillance use cases in mind. There simply isn't a smoking-gun document out there (at least not yet) which has been leaked to WikiLeaks or other credible sources, and which states that this is the case.

What can be said for certain is that if the likes of the NSA wanted to put a backdoor into every PC on the planet, the Intel Management Engine is how they would do it. It is even on record that the NSA itself mandates that the IME is disabled on any Intel PC deployed by the agency. Existing cybersecurity threats which make it possible for bad actors to use the IME as a backdoor into Intel-powered machines are also out there in the wild already. This being the case, the IME is a backdoor in all but official name.

Intel and the Andrew Tanenbaum Affair

One more thing we know about the IME is that its initial development was shrouded in secrecy. We know this thanks to Andrew Tanenbaum, a Dutch computer scientist and professor emeritus at Vrije Universiteit.

In the 1980s, Tanenbaum developed Minix, a microkernel (meaning extremely small) Linux based operating system which Intel is now known to have repurposed to use as the operating system of the IME subsystem. While never asked for his permission to repurpose Minix for this purpose, Tanenbaum claims that he was contacted by Intel several times prior to the IME's release.

Intel never told Tanenbaum what they intended to do with Minix. They simply asked him for advice concerning whether or not it was possible to make the footprint of the operating system even smaller than it was already. When Tanenbaum later discovered what Intel was really doing with Minix, he stated the following to set the record straight regarding his accidental involvement in the development of the Intel Management Engine:

> ***"For the record, I would like to state that when Intel contacted me, they didn't say what they were working on. Companies rarely talk about future products without NDAs. I figured it was a new Ethernet chip or graphics chip or something like that. If I had suspected they might be building a spy engine, I certainly wouldn't have cooperated."***

What Does the Existence of the Intel Management Engine Mean for Cryptocurrency?

Why the Intel Management Engine should concern cryptocurrency hodlers, traders, and investors is simple.

As already discussed, Satoshi Nakamoto simply couldn't comprehend the kind of cybersecurity landscape we live in today. His core vision was one which envisioned every Bitcoin miner, holder, or investor in digital currency having 100% control over the device storing their Bitcoin. As Satoshi saw it, your computer was going to be your bank.

Sadly, the reality today is that if you store any cryptocurrency on any machine using a post-2008 Intel processor, your bank backdoor isn't just wide open. It's flapping wildly in the wind, just waiting for someone to come along and take a peek inside. There is also absolutely nothing you can do to try and bolt that backdoor shut.

Today, of course, we don't just store Bitcoin or other cryptocurrencies on our laptops or home computers. We have hardware wallets and alternative CPUs like AMD and ARM processors which power our computers, phones, and ever greater numbers of so-called "smart" home appliances.

Sadly, ARM processors—which are the processors of choice for most cryptocurrency hardware wallets—and all AMD processors for at least the past five years have all shipped with their own versions of Intel's Management Engine. ARM processors use embedded technology called TrustZone, and AMD processors all ship with an embedded subsystem called the AMD Platform Security Processor. Both subsystems differ slightly in terms of their architecture and full range of capabilities. However, both essentially mirror the core functionality of the Intel Management Engine.

Every Form of Cryptocurrency Is Compromised

In The Crypto Con, I have repeatedly made clear that cryptocurrencies like Bitcoin are just software programs. Individual cryptocurrency balances are always encrypted by pairs of public and private encryption keys. However, whether keys are encrypted or not doesn't matter when a subsystem embedded in the device you use to store your digital currency can bypass any level of security to access stored data—even remotely.

It is also entirely possible that bad actors might one day use exploits in such subsystems to create botnets capable of disrupting the basic operation of cryptocurrencies like Bitcoin. The second anyone controls 51% of all computers mining Bitcoin, they can begin invalidating transactions and redistributing Bitcoin balances at will.

Even if you store cryptocurrency in a hardware wallet, a 51% attack could see attack perpetrators simply reverse the Bitcoin transaction on the Bitcoin blockchain which saw you first send your Bitcoin balance to the address of your hardware wallet in the first place.

Put simply, no form of cryptocurrency can be stored safely anywhere.

The Ghost in the Internet Machine

People in general don't like bad news. A comfortable kind of cognitive dissonance sees even leading cybersecurity researchers ignore the very existence of subsystems like the Intel Management Engine. Some even triumph such subsystems as being integral to contemporary cybersecurity. However, these subsystems exist, exploits to them are out there in the internet ether, and their very existence is a clear and credible threat to cryptocurrency.

People like Andrew Tanenbaum, who was tricked into helping create Intel's ghost in the machine, know this—and now so do you.

Nudge Nudge - How Governments Are Using Behavioral Insights to Encourage Us to Go Cashless

Is Bitcoin really the product of a one-man grassroots financial revolution that is still in progress? Or was Bitcoin always just a global psychological operation perpetrated by some secretive agency like the NSA?

So far in The Crypto Con, I've demonstrated how Bitcoin and possibly some people integral to Bitcoin's early adoption were seemingly protected by agencies like the NSA and FBI. I've also demonstrated how technology present in almost all modern computers since 2008 negates even the best cryptocurrency security practices. The only question is, if Bitcoin was created by the likes of the CIA, what was the point?

To understand why Bitcoin might have been created by the likes of the CIA or NSA, it is first necessary to step back in time to the pre-Bitcoin era of cryptocurrency and even currency itself.

The Pre-Bitcoin Era of Digital Currency

The world is bankrupt, and it has been for a long time. It wasn't always this way, though.

Once upon a time, most of the world economy was based on a system of representative money first implemented in China, and later brought to Europe by none other than Marco Polo.

On his travels in the Orient, Marco Polo discovered that rather than use physical gold and silver in day-to-day commerce, the Chinese used a system where paper credit notes representative of real gold held by the Emperor Kublai Khan's mint in the city of Cambaluc were used in trade instead. All notes were stamped with the seal of the Emperor, and should notes start to become ruined, they could be taken back to Cambaluc where holders could pay 3% of their value to have them replaced.

Porting this monetary invention to his home of Venice in 1295 subsequently sparked the start of the Renaissance. Italy became integral to renewed trade with the Orient, and paper representative of precious metals like gold and silver became the standard means of exchange all across Europe.

The age of representative money only ended in 1971, when President Nixon officially ended the direct convertibility of the U.S. dollar to gold. This ushered in the modern era of fractional reserve banking, which sees banks hold only a fraction of customer deposits. The bulk of the remainder of consumer deposits being used for commercial lending and investing.

The basic premise of fractional reserve banking is that new money will be created by interest repayable on loans and eventual returns on investments. This will, in theory, increase the existing money supply. However, any interest or returns on investments only ever exists as digital money on a screen. Neither is this new money representative of anything like gold or silver. Since 1971, the financial world has subsequently been spiraling toward a new, purely digital currency metaphor.

To put this in perspective, at the time of writing, the U.S. government is in over $38 trillion of debt. However, there are approximately only $2 trillion worth of U.S. dollar notes in global circulation. What this means is that even if a small percentage of Americans attempt to ever withdraw the entirety of their U.S. bank balances, there will be an immediate and quite catastrophic financial collapse.

The only way to prevent such a collapse from eventually happening is to transition to a purely digital currency.

Major banks and businesses began trialing such digital currencies from as early as the 1980s. One of the first of these was 1989's DigiCash. Like Bitcoin, DigiCash was digitally minted, and complex encryption prevented double spending while also making transactions anonymous. DigiCash's creator, David Chaum, also partnered with major banks. This saw users be able to easily convert real cash into DigiCash.

Other early precursors to Bitcoin include E-Gold, Bit Gold, and B-Money. All, though, suffered from the same problem. All used a centralized ledger like a regular bank ledger to confirm transactions, and overall adoption was lackluster. No one, not even the tech-savvy Japanese, were interested in anyone trying to sell them gimmicky e-cash.

Subconsciously, people seemed to understand that no matter how hard the sell was, they wouldn't ever have money again if you ever took physical cash out of their hand. Then in 1996, something interesting happened.

On October 31, 1996, the U.S. National Security Agency (NSA)—yes, them again—published a white paper titled:

"How to Make a Mint: Cryptography of Anonymous Electronic Cash."

The paper itself is a deep dive into the potential world of digital currency. In it, what was essentially a rewrite of David Chaum's original vision for digital currency is presented, before the stripping out of things like transaction anonymity and user privacy. The NSA itself even argued that digital currency should have a decentralized, rather than centralized, transaction ledger.

Why would they do that? Well, it was already clear that the masses would never really trust a centralized digital money system. If you wanted a monetary revolution or switch of a current monetary metaphor, it was always going to have to look organic. After all, in the immortal words of Margaret Mead:

"Never doubt that a small group of thoughtful, committed citizens can change the world; indeed, it's the only thing that ever has."

If Bitcoin has always been a psychological operation perpetrated by the NSA, it has been brilliantly executed.

Rather than presenting Bitcoin to the world, the NSA simply seeded the Bitcoin forum and waited for Bitcoin to be organically stumbled upon by the masses. When this finally happened, banks and world governments warned people against investing in the digital currency. However, thanks to the Streisand effect and the basic rules of reverse psychology, warning people against Bitcoin only resulted in an explosion of online interest in the fledgling cryptocurrency.

The idea was simple. Don't push digital currency on the world. Make the world want it, and what better way to do that than by designing a cryptocurrency that supposedly gave a middle finger to THE MAN and, even better, would make its early adopters incredibly wealthy?

The only question is, are we living in a new monetary Renaissance? Or are we being quietly nudged toward accepting a wholly hellish new financial paradigm?

What Exactly Is Nudging?

The concept of nudging originates in a 2008 book called ***Nudge: Improving Decisions about Health, Wealth, and Happiness***, by behavioral economist Richard Thaler and Harvard Law Professor Cass Sunstein.

In Nudge, Thaler and Sunstein make it clear that they believe people generally behave irrationally. As a result, the average member of the public is incapable of smart decision-making. Thankfully, this can be countered (they argue) by having a third party act as an architect who reframes people's perceptions of the choices available to them.

To demonstrate, we need only look at the success of the UK's dedicated Nudge Unit (and yes, this is a real thing) in adding more people to the UK organ donor register.

Put simply, when members of the public were encouraged to opt in to being organ donors, the majority of people didn't. However, when the government made it obligatory to opt out of being a donor, an extraordinarily small number of people chose to do so. As a result, the vast majority of UK residents are now on the organ donor register, all thanks to the way the government and its Nudge Unit reframed how people agree to be on this register.

Usually, governments don't openly advertise how they use nudge units and behavioral insights teams. However, we do know that at present the official UK nudge unit is using nudging to reframe the general population's perception of heat pump technology.

ANDREW BRASSELL

The UK Government's Heat Pump Hard Sell

The UK government has a problem. At present, the cost of electricity in the United Kingdom is almost quadruple the cost of natural gas. In fact, the average Brit pays at least a third more for their electricity than people in Europe and North America. This is a problem, as to become carbon neutral by 2050, the UK government wants everyone to stop using gas to heat their homes. Instead, they want everyone to transition to using more environmentally friendly electric heat pumps.

Sad0ly, because heat pumps cost more to run in the long term than existing gas boilers, few Brits are willing to abandon their trusty gas boilers just yet. This is why the UK government is putting its morally dubious behavioral insights team on the case.

In the case of the UK government's current heat pump dilemma, the answer from the UK government's behavioral insights team is to reframe any negative chatter online about heat pumps as simple disinformation. It does not matter if newer gas boiler models really are cheaper and less costly to operate (at least in the UK). As far as the UK government and its Nudge Unit are concerned, all such talk should be framed as disinformation spread by legacy gas boiler manufacturers. That's just one form of nudge, though.

In tandem with the UK government attempting to reframe any talk of conventional gas boilers being less costly to run than heat pumps, they have also launched a direct attack on users of wood-burning stoves.

To demonstrate, each week, major newspapers and online news portals like the Daily Mail publish new sensationalized wood stove horror stories. Just a few headlines from 2025 include:

- Wood burners linked to 2,500 deaths a year in the UK, study claims

- Wood burning stoves undermining air pollution fight, figures show

- Trendy indoor wood burning stoves are as bad for the lungs as smoking...

- A trendy wood burning stove almost killed me... they need to be banned

- Wood burning stove warning as new study proves lung damage 'like...

There are also currently groups like "Mums for Lungs," an apparently grassroots organization, pressuring the UK government to ban wood stoves. There is just one problem.

In Brixton, where Mums for Lungs are located, you would usually have to travel approximately 200 or 300 miles to find more than a handful of people using wood-burning stoves. The vast majority of people using wood stoves in the UK in this day and age are, after all, people in off-grid locations like the Welsh mountains and the wilds of the Scottish Highlands. They're not in Brixton, where Mums for Lungs is located and are apparently so concerned about children coming into contact with woodsmoke that they want to ban everyone, anywhere, from ever lighting a wood fire.

For the sake of perspective, there were 1,887 instances of knife crime in Brixton in the first six months of 2025. I, personally, would therefore be more worried about any child I raised there being stabbed to death, but what do I know? Apparently, it's woodsmoke that parents should be worried about.

All of this, in short, is nudging. Some of the fiercest resistance to heat pumps in the UK, after all, comes from communities in remote areas where peat, coal, and wood is still used to heat homes due to there being no sufficient mains gas or electricity supply.

Nudging Is a Global Phenomenon

The UK government isn't the only government in the world to utilize behavioral insights and nudging to acclimatize populations slowly to new social and economic realities. Rather, the World Bank has its very own behavioral sciences team. In the World Bank's own words:

"The Mind, Behavior, and Development Unit (eMBeD), the World Bank's behavioral sciences team, works closely with project teams, governments, and other partners to diagnose, design, and evaluate behaviorally informed interventions. By collaborating with a worldwide network of scientists and practitioners, the eMBeD team provides answers to important economic and social questions, and contributes to the global effort to eliminate poverty and increase equity."

Of course, when the World Bank markets its use of behavioral insights teams and nudging to address poverty and inequality, this makes nudging sound wholly positive. However, the reality on the ground in several African countries is that fighting poverty typically sees groups like the World Bank Group, Bill & Melinda Gates Foundation, and the Commonwealth & Development Office (among others) incentivize local populations to adopt cashless payment systems, e-money, and digital tokenization of physical commodities.

It is, of course, easy to incentivize entire populations to do away with physical cash completely when cash is already scarce to begin with. However, it is not so easy in Western countries. That's why, in places like the UK, nudging starts to become more of a hard shove toward acceptance of a new financial status quo.

To demonstrate, in a 2009 paper titled ***"Could Nudges Steer Us Towards a Cashless Society?,"*** its author, Leo Van Hove, Professor of Economics at the University of Brussels, explicitly mentions e-purses and electronic wallets, despite Bitcoin and the very concept of cryptocurrency being unknown to all but a handful of people at the time.

In Van Hove's 2009 paper, he also theorized how governments might start nudging populations to accept cashless payments, specifically by "increasing the hassle factor" of using cash. He even theorized that banks themselves might assist in this aggravated form of nudging.

Fast forward to the present, and bank closures and ever scarcer numbers of ATMs in the Republic of Ireland have been proven to be part of a banking industry-wide push to encourage people to rely more on cashless payments.

In Ireland, the Irish Financial Services Union (FSU) discovered that several banks have intentionally implemented a policy of understaffing bank branches and even intentionally refusing to answer telephones to create long queues that frustrate customers. The FSU also found that banks are intentionally slow to fix faulty in-branch ATMs. Often, when an ATM fails, it will be removed completely with no plans for replacement. This has led to hundreds of new ATMs being bought by private-sector actors who charge high fees for withdrawals.

Across the banking industry, the FSU found that even competing banks are collaborating to discourage members of the public from using cash and brick-and-mortar branches, in favor of cashless payments and wholly online banking services.

While not officially acknowledged like in Ireland, the same "increasing of the hassle factor" of using cash, as suggested by Van Hove, can be seen all across the UK and Europe. On the surface, bank closures and fewer ATMs are suggested to be the result of high operating costs and falling foot traffic in physical bank branches. In reality, though, branch closures and restricted ATM access are all part of industry-coordinated psychological nudging.

The Bitcoin Carrot & The Banking Stick

One of the fundamental things to remember when looking at how governments and financial institutions routinely nudge us to go cashless is that if this happens, the money in your bank won't be the same as it is today. Neither will it be anything like Bitcoin.

To play Devil's advocate, it can be argued to make perfect sense to do away with most bank branches and even ATMs. After all, most of the legacy banking services people are familiar with can be easily accessed online and through apps. However, the digital money which you see on a screen today when checking your balance via an app or online banking portal is not the same as the digital money you will see in the cashless world which society is slowly being nudged toward.

It is not just physical paper cash which the financial hierarchy of the world wants to resign to obsolescence like yesteryear's representative cash.

Whether cryptocurrency was invented by a genuine genius financial martyr or the NSA doesn't matter. Cryptocurrency, unlike today's cash that is just numbers on a screen, is programmable, traceable, and ingeniously versatile. This is why the ultimate, (and publicly stated goal of the leaders of the UK and EU), is to gradually start replacing cash by 2030 with Central Bank Digital Currencies (CBDCs).

Unlike the cash in your bank today, banks will be able to dictate where and how you spend your CBDC balance. If they want, they will even be able to put expiry dates on CBDC balances. This will see some or all of your latest paycheck expire after a certain amount of time if you haven't spent it already. Your every transaction will also be monitored, and you can say goodbye completely to cash-in-hand side hustles like yard sales or doing an odd job for a friend. Every single penny you ever acquire will be taxable.

CBDCs, in short, are wholly different from cryptocurrencies like Bitcoin. For one, transactions will be processed via a centrally administered transaction ledger, which—as we've already discussed—was why the first forms of cryptocurrency from the pre-Bitcoin era never became a mainstream hit. And if you think about it, that's how the big Bitcoin nudge might have always been designed to work.

Once upon a time in 2008, a Japanese man came to dangle a carrot called Bitcoin before the donkey of humanity. "This will make you rich. This will free you from monetary enslavement to THE MAN," he said.

Meanwhile, behind the donkey of humanity, THE MAN began hitting the donkey with the stick of inflation, bank closures, ATMs becoming scarcer, and online banking.

All the donkey didn't know was that the man with the carrot and THE MAN with the stick were always the same person, and that the donkey itself was always being nudged to go in the same hellish direction.

What Are CBDCs? – Tomorrow's Nightmare Money Explained

In The Crypto Con, I have so far made it clear that I believe digital currencies such as Bitcoin might be nothing more than a massive global psy-op.

The mainstream media encourages us to believe that Bitcoin emerged thanks to the work of a single anonymous individual, the now-infamous Satoshi Nakamoto, who to date hasn't made a penny profit from his creation. Likewise, the same mainstream media encourages us to believe that the emergence of other altcoins, which now make up a $4 trillion+ digital currency market, has been a 100% grassroots, community-driven response to the arrival of Bitcoin.

Sadly, I'm a little cynical.

My belief is that one or more three-letter government agencies, like the CIA and NSA, are the real founding fathers of the current cryptocurrency movement. It is also my belief that the gradual popularization of cryptocurrency is nothing more than a purposeful attempt to slowly condition society to accept a completely cashless future. More specifically, a future where the majority of Western fiat currencies (the currencies we use today) are superseded by Central Bank Digital Currencies (CBDCs). The only question is, what are CBDCs?

What Are Central Bank Digital Currencies?

Imagine if every penny you ever spent, from womb to tomb, was traceable back to you. With CBDCs, this will not just be possible; it will be a key feature integral to the basic functioning of every digital penny that ever graces your bank account.

Just like how today every Bitcoin transaction can be traced back to the mining of the original Bitcoin genesis block by Satoshi Nakamoto in 2009, every CBDC cent you ever acquire will be traceable to its original source. Every penny will also be scrutinized as you acquire it. Did someone outside of your known social circle just send money to your bank account? If so, why? Did you sell something to somebody online? Is this a taxable event?

Are you a young person regularly relying on the bank of mum and dad to help pay the extortionate rent on your matchbox apartment? If so, should such regular deposits into your bank be considered taxable income? Moreover, if you receive any kind of government assistance, should this now be automatically reduced as it is clear you have alternative means of financial assistance?

Make no mistake, central bank digital currencies will build on all the best features of today's leading cryptocurrencies. You will be able to send and receive money instantly from anywhere in the world. They will eventually be biometrically linked to unique physical characteristics like your iris pattern, making theft and fraud nearly impossible. They will even eventually be linked to real tokenized assets that you own, like physical property.

Fallen on hard times? Don't worry. In just a few taps of an app on your phone, you will be able to release some of the equity from your home that is already stored on a blockchain somewhere without requiring any intermediary. Need a loan? As CBDCs will link directly to your digital identity—meaning your health, education, employment, credit record, and even voting history—you will be able to qualify in seconds. However, the benefits end here.

The Nightmare CBDC Metaverse of Constant Metadata Analysis

At present, there are limits to how much your bank knows about you. However, in the coming central bank digital currency era, your bank will know before your spouse or boyfriend if you think you might be pregnant. They will ascertain this the second you buy a pregnancy test. Having an affair? They'll know all about that too. Why else would you be regularly checking in to that motel you hook up at, while it is clear from your wife's financial metadata that she's usually at home at the same time ordering takeout from Uber Eats?

If you are having an affair, might the possible revelation of this leave you or your spouse unable to keep up with mortgage payments? If the bank AI analyzing your spending habits and associated metadata says yes, maybe it will up your rate to offset potential future defaults.

When your entire financial life is governed by meticulous analysis of every byte of metadata linked to your associated digital identity, there are no such things as secrets. In fact, George Orwell isn't just spinning in his grave when it comes to the privacy nightmare of CBDCs. Rather, he's just taken off in a Black Hawk helicopter.

As Catherine Austin Fitts, former United States Assistant Secretary of Housing, puts it, CBDCs are the complete antithesis of cash as we currently know it. Rather than being a convenient digital replacement for cash, CBDCs represent a new "control grid" form of currency, one designed to give central banks and governments unprecedented authority over how, when, and where money is used.

Make no mistake, where cryptocurrencies like Bitcoin might have been created to empower people to regain financial sovereignty over their own lives, central bank digital currencies are all about creating a financial human ant farm.

Do you owe fines, penalties, or taxes? If so, these will simply be deducted automatically from your CBDC balance. Alternatively, you might be prohibited from using your CBDC balance to travel any further than your known workplace until whatever money you owe is repaid. Work from home? Hopefully, you've got a good view. You might be staying there a while.

CBDCs Are Already in Active Development

If you are not worried about how CBDCs might one day impede your financial freedom, you should be. For several years already, institutions like the Bank for International Settlements (BIS), based in Basel, Switzerland, have been working with major central banks, including the European Central Bank and Federal Reserve, to prototype and test CBDCs worldwide. This is despite assurances by the likes of the current Trump administration in the U.S. that a CBDC implementation of the dollar isn't open for discussion.

Of course, banks and governments can already impose fines and liens, as well as make direct deductions from income at source. However, at present, when you swipe your card in a grocery store, your bank or credit card issuer merely validates whether you have enough credit or money in your account to cover the cost of a transaction. By comparison, and as made clear by Bo Li, former Deputy Managing Director of the International Monetary Fund, future central bank digital currencies will be programmable. In effect, your money won't be money anymore; it will be software.

This means that although you may have enough money in your account to settle a grocery store bill, future transactions may be declined if you have been preemptively restricted from purchasing certain goods or services.

Programmability, even at a basic level, allows central banks and governments to embed specific rules and conditions into currency itself. CBDC transactions can subsequently be programmed to restrict usage to certain purposes, such as food purchases or welfare payments, or to limit transactions based on geographic location, time, or compliance with government mandates. This capability is enabled by advanced technologies like artificial intelligence (AI) and cloud computing, which allow for real-time monitoring and enforcement of these rules.

No Constitution Will Ever Protect You From CBDC Tyranny

To get a taste of what CBDCs will eventually mean for society, we need only look back in time to the Canadian trucker protests of 2022.

To protest government vaccine mandates, big rig truckers in Canada converged in Ottawa and blockaded border crossings. In response, the Canadian government used Canada's Emergency Act to justify the freezing of protesters' bank accounts and even the freezing of funds from wider community fundraising efforts intended to support protesters.

It then took until 2024 for Canadian Federal Court Justice Richard Mosley to rule that the invocation of the Emergencies Act in this way was unreasonable and led to a direct infringement of truckers' constitutional rights.

The lesson here is simple. Even today, democratic governments have the power to de-bank anyone they like. (Remember, we also saw this with WikiLeaks.)

It can then take years of battling bureaucracy to hold governments to account, by which time damage to individual rights, civil liberties, and basic financial freedoms has already been done. What hope is there then for democracy or civil society, when governments don't even need to activate emergency powers to freeze your bank account? With programmable CBDCs at their disposal, they will be able to disperse protests simply by making it impossible for people to buy essentials like food and water in protest locations.

It is also important to remember that money itself isn't issued or even controlled by the governments we elect. The Federal Reserve, Bank of England, and European Central Bank all operate in a democratic grey zone. They profess not to be private banks, yet they all have almost full autonomy over their own governance. They adjust interest rates independently of governments, they oversee the payment systems we use, and they issue every penny of the digital and physical currencies we use.

As their name suggests, it will be Central Banks like the Federal Reserve and ECB who will issue the Central Bank Digital Currencies with which cash as we know it today will eventually be replaced. They will subsequently pull the levers of control of their new nightmare money, not any democratically elected government.

One Rule for You – Another for the Powers Governing You

The greatest risk that CBDCs impose on populations lies in the fact that future Central Bank Digital Currencies will be linked directly to individual digital identities. These are not just digital versions of passports, driver's licenses, and national ID cards. Rather, we're talking about centralized ID databases which verify individuals via the social media accounts they use, their medical records, their academic records, vaccine records, travel and military service records, and even workplace training records.

The goal will be to create a complete digital profile of every CBDC user to predict and augment their spending habits, as well as offset risk when issuing the likes of loans.

Did you serve in the last war but later question the lack of services for veterans or even the legitimacy of the war itself? If so, you may be restricted from buying firearms or donating to certain charities or political causes because your donation might be flagged as having an unfair risk of bias.

Are you looking to secure a loan to start a business or buy a home, but have a habit of indulging in junk food? If so, is there any chance that you might succumb to cancer or heart disease, as evidence shows your parents did or your now-public (and it is now public) 23andMe DNA profile shows your ancestors did, before your loan will be repaid?

Make no mistake: CBDCs aren't equivalents of the digital cash you see on a screen today or the get-rich-quick cryptocurrencies you keep hearing others talk about.

CBDCs are only called digital currencies to make them sound similar to cryptocurrencies like Bitcoin. In reality, they are an entirely new form of smart money, which issuing banks will always presume to know how to spend better for your benefit than you do. That said, the same rules that apply to you don't apply to them.

In the United States, fiscal rules like the Federal Accounting Standards Advisory Board Statement 56 (FASAB 56), implemented in 2018, already exist. This rule allows the U.S. federal government to obscure portions of its financial statements through secretive processes. This rule is also how over $21 trillion in undocumented adjustments identified in federal accounts since 1998 has simply been made to vanish into thin air. (Keep in mind that the U.S. is currently in $38 trillion+ of national debt.)

Put simply, CBDCs will give governments and central banks the ability to scrutinize and possibly restrict every penny you ever spend in the name of fighting terror, climate change, tax avoidance, election fraud, and even financial inequality. However, you will never be able to hold banks or governments accountable for holes in their own budgets, no matter how massive.

Let's Not Talk About the Elephant in the Room

In case I haven't been 100% clear, there is no physical cash in a CBDC economy. There is no such thing as an emergency fiver squirreled away somewhere that you can turn to when you are broke.

In a CBDC future, physical cash is just a souvenir from yesteryear. It holds no value. One question must, therefore, be asked: Namely, what happens to the economy during a power outage or an attack on or failure of the basic IT infrastructure required to keep the future CBDC economy running? As it stands, the proverbial powers that be have no answer to this question.

Unlike how today the cash economy can still function during the likes of a power outage, the CBDC world of tomorrow will grind to a halt the second your phone needs charging, or the second a lightning strike takes out an electric substation somewhere. The CBDC economy of tomorrow is also one which has no need of legacy cryptocurrencies like Bitcoin.

The minute news gets out that you can use your CBDC balance to buy Bitcoin and still buy and sell basic goods and services as pseudonymously as you once did with cash, you can be sure that Bitcoin and other legacy cryptocurrencies will be just as unceremoniously consigned to history the same way that representative cash and regular cash as we know it is about to be.

Where's Daddy? - Nightmare Metadata Analysis in Action

In The Crypto Con, I've attempted to gently shake readers free of the mass cognitive dissonance which many of us, especially in the West, have concerning modern technology.

Every day, we use devices and apps which many of us consider essential for being able to function in modern society. Thanks to bright colors, emojis, memes, and of course, occasional cat videos, we regard such apps as harmless extensions of our intrinsic social nature. Today, we are even at a point in the evolution of our relationship with technology, which sees people turn first to AI agents like ChatGPT for everything from legal advice to relationship advice, before we ever consider turning to a real human.

Sadly, what the vast majority of people don't realize when utilizing such technologies, is the fact that the corporations behind such social media and AI platforms are far from passive providers of wholesome new ways to connect.

Where's Daddy?

Regardless of anyone's personal opinion of the 2023 until present (at the time of writing) conflict in Gaza, one thing is without question. This being that the start of the conflict in October 2023, was the start of the world's first AI-powered conflict.

Google, the friendly provider of most of the world's email, Microsoft, and Amazon Web Services, are silent, albeit proven partners with the Israeli Defense Force. Willingly, they provide server space and cloud computing services which are used to deliver a range of OpenAI-derived artificial intelligence services. (OpenAI being the creators of ChatGPT).

OpenAI-derived systems known to be in use in the conflict in Gaza include AI systems with codenames like "Lavender," "The Gospel," and "Where's Daddy?"

Rumored to incorporate metadata from WhatsApp and possibly Google, Where's Daddy is an AI system which tracks the real-time location of suspected enemy combatant cellphones. If a suspected enemy combatant returns to a known address of an enemy combatant, Where's Daddy takes this as a confirmation of identity and the IDF carries out a precision strike on the home in question.

Homes become kill rooms, women and children become pre-calculated collateral damage, and any civilians housed in the same apartment building or the same tent encampment become acceptable losses. Meanwhile, on the other side of the Atlantic, users of OpenAI services like ChatGPT are busy using ChatGPT apps on their phones to cheat on school homework and ask what the price of Bitcoin will be in 2030.

There has never been a greater state of technological ignorance in the entirety of the history of humanity.

In places like America, social media empowers people like social justice warriors to protest injustice and overreach of government. Meanwhile, the very same platforms aid in real-time target practice of suspected militants in places like Palestine. Worse, it's AI targeting systems like Lavender which decide if someone is a suspected militant or not—not a real human. This is made possible by almost three decades of intensive metadata analysis of basic human behavior, right down to analysis of different gaits which people subconsciously adopt when walking.

To really understand this nightmare story of metadata analysis, though, we must first go back to the early 2000s.

Social Media & The Total Information Awareness Trap

In a New York Times 2002 Opinion Piece by William Safire titled: You Are Suspect, Safire stated the following:

- "If the Homeland Security Act is not amended before passage, here is what will happen to you:

- Every purchase you make with a credit card, every magazine subscription you buy and medical prescription you fill, every website you visit and email you send or receive, every academic grade you receive, every bank deposit you make, every trip you book and every event you attend—all these transactions and communications will go into what the Defense Department describes as "a virtual, centralized, grand database" about every U.S. citizen."

At the time, America's Defense Advanced Research Projects Agency, (DARPA) was attempting to create a "precrime" approach to combatting terrorism known as Total Information Awareness (TIA). This was a database which would create a profile of every U.S. citizen, while also creating secondary databases of every citizen's known social contacts. The TIA database would also strive to know everything about everyone, from what books you checked out of the library, to what porn you just looked at online.

Thanks to people like William Safire, DARPA's proposed TIA system met with increasing citizen outrage. This saw the official TIA project be broken up among different DARPA departments, one of which became an MIT—Massachusetts Institute of Technology—project called LifeLog.

Persisting until 2004, proponents of LifeLog were quick to advance the idea that having full-spectrum knowledge about people's lives and behavior was an inherently good thing. With LifeLog, it would be possible to track and predict the spread of future pandemics. Total information awareness would also make it possible to one day create state-of-the-art AI assistants and avatars to assist members of the public with everyday tasks. This being thanks to the coalescence of an endless ocean of human knowledge and metadata. (And remember this is 2004, not 2024).

Sadly for LifeLog, persisting citizen privacy concerns about what was still a DARPA pet project saw LifeLog and all associated DARPA projects shuttered completely on the 4th of February 2004. Just coincidentally, though, the 4th of February 2004 was the same date a little something called TheFacebook was launched, before being rebranded a year later, to just Facebook.

Once again, the powers that be had realized that the general public would never accept the government collecting data on (as the New York Times reported): "all of a subject's experience, from phone numbers dialed and email messages viewed to every breath taken, step made and place gone."

This being the case, LifeLog quietly became Facebook, a friendly new social media platform sold to the public as an easy way to stay connected to friends and family. Naturally, Facebook would harvest as much data as it possibly could about users in the same way LifeLog wanted to. However, as long as users believed that Facebook was created by a random computer nerd and they never bothered to read the small print stating how their data would be used by third parties, this didn't matter.

Blurring of Battle Lines & The Crypto Long Con

In Europe and the United Kingdom, Central Bank Digital Currencies are planned to launch no later than 2030. When they do, the vast majority of the public will be led to believe that their arrival is thanks to new technological innovations. This and that their rollout is likely the only possible solution to some existential financial threat.

In reality, none of humanity's technological innovations from the past thirty years have really happened by chance or grassroots coincidence. For central bank digital currencies to work the way central banks want them to, they will require vast amounts of individual metadata and the ability to analyze this data in real time. Social media was, therefore, given to us by DARPA so that humanity would effectively gift DARPA back all the metadata it could ever want.

Thanks to analysis of this metadata, we now have AI language models and software-based neural networks capable of exactly the kind of real-time analysis of vast amounts of data necessary in the coming age of CBDCs. Where today, such AIs analyze real-time drone footage of Palestinians to determine who might be justifiable military target, tomorrow will see similar systems identify people dropping litter in Times Square, before automatically deducting fines from their CBDC bank balances.—Of course, the powers that be will likely wait a while before CBDCs are used to such an overt 1984 nightmare extent.

As of 2025, we also have cryptocurrencies like Bitcoin which have been operating autonomously in the wild for almost two decades. This proves to the masses that cryptocurrency as a concept doesn't just work. Rather, it apparently works better than the currency we know. After all, holding a handful of dollars for two decades doesn't usually make anyone a millionaire. Thanks to inflation, it usually just makes people poorer. CBDCs won't make anyone rich, but the idea that cryptocurrency will is now embedded in the human psyche and this is all that matters.

As of 2025, we also now have a blurring of the final lines between cryptocurrency, social media, and AI.

Ever since the arrival of Bitcoin in 2009, critics have decried how power-hungry cryptocurrency is. This is thanks to the kilowatts of electricity required to run the average Bitcoin mining farm. Now, however, social media giants like Google are signing billion-dollar deals with Bitcoin mining farms, thanks to their ability to be simultaneously used as data centers already equipped with enough raw computational power to run the latest, most state-of-the-art AI models.

Where's Daddy?

Where the human race is right now, isn't the best place it could be. While the social media metadata-fueled AIs we don't know we helped passively create help hunt Palestinians, we're also spiraling toward a new kind of purely digital currency nightmare era which we will probably celebrate when it arrives.

We are ignorant to what the future holds. Someone out there isn't, though. If he was ever real and if he was ever as authentic, altruistic, and as brilliant as the Bitcoin community assumes he was, a man called Satoshi Nakamoto would rise up right now to tell us that we're using his invention to go in completely the wrong direction. This being the case, where is he?

Where is Satoshi Nakamoto? Where the hell is daddy?

Satoshi Nakamoto Never Existed

It's been the greatest nerd hunt of the 21st century. Who is, or who was, Satoshi Nakamoto? As nerd hunts go, though, the search for Satoshi has also been something of a non-starter. For several years, names like Hal Finney, Nick Szabo, Adam Back, and even that of the great Satoshi impostor Craig Wright have been recycled over and over in an ever-repeating game of Bitcoin Guess Who.

Only rarely does anyone dive into the Satoshi Nakamoto mythos, only to resurface to boldly say: "Hey, what if Satoshi just never existed in the first place?"

The Satoshi Nakamoto Origin Story

In 2008, and to simplify Satoshi Nakamoto's origin story as concisely as possible, someone, or some group, went to great lengths to anonymously establish several ultra-secure email addresses before also registering the domain name bitcoin.org just as anonymously.

To this day, no one is 100% certain how Satoshi was able to register the bitcoin.org domain without leaving a single financial fingerprint. Even today, this isn't possible when registering a domain using Bitcoin as a payment medium. However, we do know that one email provider Satoshi was using, anonymousspeech.com, was able to take payment for new email services in E-Gold. (E-Gold being a now-defunct precursor to contemporary cryptocurrency.)

Anyone anywhere can also verify via Whois.com that bitcoin.org was initially registered to Anonymousspeech LLC. This implies that Satoshi and a Swiss national by the name of Michael Niklaus Weber, the founder of Anonymousspeech, may have collaborated in some way to secure bitcoin.org. The other obvious inference is that Satoshi Nakamoto himself was always Michael Niklaus Weber.

In either case, the steps which Satoshi took to communicate via only ultra-secure email providers, third-party domain registrars, and services like Tor (right from the beginning of his appearance online) suggest that Satoshi was keenly aware of the surveillance powers of agencies like the NSA. This is despite the fact that it would be four more years before the scope of such powers would be exposed by Edward Snowden.

Satoshi Secures His Scapegoats

Today, names like Gavin Andresen, Hal Finney, and Adam Back are often recycled by investigators into the true identity of Satoshi Nakamoto. This is thanks to many of the people who first participated in the Bitcoin network all appearing on the Bitcoin scene at the exact same time. However, this didn't happen by accident. Rather, on August 18, 2008, after Satoshi successfully registered bitcoin.org, he quickly got to work turning his domain into a cryptography-centric forum which still exists today in the form of bitcointalk.org.

On the surface, the aim of bitcoin.org was to give fellow cryptographers a place to review Satoshi's work on Bitcoin. There was just one problem. It can take weeks, if not months, for a new forum to populate organically. Satoshi, therefore, used the previously discussed cyberpunk mailing list operated by the website metzdowd.com to draw the attention of several experts in the field of cryptography directly to his project.

Drawing direct attention to bitcoin.org in this way proved successful. Think of a name today connected with Bitcoin, and you'll likely find the same name on the original Bitcoin mailing list.

In retrospect, it also seems to be the case that Satoshi was making plans to disappear right from the start. A second goal of bitcoin.org, therefore, seems to have been to find people who would continue to maintain and represent Bitcoin in the event of Satoshi going AWOL.

We see evidence of this in Satoshi Nakamoto's immediate trust in people like the Icelandic college student Martti Malmi.

Shortly after discovering bitcoin.org, Malmi was able to impress Satoshi with his ability to explain the underlying premise of Bitcoin better than Satoshi himself. Malmi subsequently took over the creation of all FAQ content on bitcoin.org, before shortly after taking over official ownership of the entire forum itself. Indeed, despite having gone to great lengths to anonymously register and create bitcoin.org, Satoshi effectively relinquished all control of his platform and convinced a real, easily traceable human to become the official face of the bitcoin.org forum less than 12 months later.

As one of the only original Bitcoin miners (if not the only miner after Satoshi), there is also a case to be made that Malmi, a child prodigy who learned to code at the age of 12, might actually be Satoshi. However, when it comes to unmasking the genius behind Satoshi Nakamoto, it quickly becomes clear that Satoshi was a master of subterfuge.

Whatever You Do, Don't Follow the Breadcrumbs

Just five months after establishing bitcoin.org, Satoshi himself began mining the Bitcoin genesis block. When he did, he left a short message in microcode within the genesis block itself, one which is preserved to this day on the Bitcoin blockchain.

"The Times 03/Jan/2009," it reads, **"Chancellor on brink of second bailout for banks."**

As Bitcoin by nature is inflation-proof and decentralized, Satoshi seemed to be saying, "Welcome to Bitcoin, the solution to the current global financial crisis." However, his use of a reference to the UK newspaper, The Times, and his use of the UK time and date format seem to also suggest that Satoshi Nakamoto himself was British.

In a way, Satoshi fired the starting gun of the greatest nerd hunt of the 21st century all by himself. Specifically, by giving the world its first real hint to his true identity. However, this message would eventually prove to be one of several carefully placed breadcrumbs, none of which really help us identify the real persona behind Nakamoto. In fact, the more breadcrumbs one discovers, the more obscure the true identity of Satoshi becomes.

- Remember Michael Niklaus Weber, the founder of anonymousspeech.com who accepted E-Gold payments and who likely assisted in the purchase of bitcoin.org? Well, at the time that bitcoin.org was registered, Weber was himself residing in Tokyo. This isn't a surprise, as Anonymousspeech LLC was then registered at a physical address in Nakano-ku, Tokyo. Weber would also later post occasionally on bitcoin.org. Whenever he did, he, like Satoshi, would appear to use British spelling and grammar; and like Satoshi, use the term "block chain," as opposed to "blockchain."

- As well as the alias "Satoshi Nakamoto" being a quite common name in Japan, it can also be translated in Chinese to mean "the wise one of the Chinese currency." Right from the start, Bitcoin mining began to consolidate in China. In fact, Chinese miners often process as much as 55% of all Bitcoin transactions, even during countrywide mining bans. Several notable people, exchanges, and cryptocurrency projects like Cardano and Tron also have their bases in

China and Hong Kong. This could imply that Satoshi was originally from China or Hong Kong, which would also explain his use of British spelling and the British time and date format.

- Those who have studied the posting behavior of Nakamoto on bitcoin.org prior to his disappearance have discovered that Satoshi's posting patterns match those of a college or university student. This is thanks to Satoshi only posting sporadically during academic term times, as opposed to more frequently between semesters.

- The penchant for embedding sneaky political messages in code, like Satoshi did with his Times newspaper headline, is one shared by another contributor to bitcoin.org, the British cryptographer Adam Back, who (at the time of writing) is the current CEO of Blockstream—Blockstream being the entity which governs updates and the occasional implementation of new features to Bitcoin's core software.

- For some reason, a full copy of the Bitcoin whitepaper has been hidden as an Easter egg in the code of every Apple computer since the release of macOS Mojave in 2018. This is despite Apple as a company having shown long-standing disinterest in participating in the Bitcoin or wider crypto ecosystem. Some, though, suggest that the whitepaper being present in macOS is evidence that Satoshi may have been an Apple software engineer or perhaps even the late great Steve Jobs.

- The bibliography of the Bitcoin whitepaper, which Satoshi released on Halloween 2008, is clumsy and disorganized. Most academics reading it would subsequently assume that whoever Satoshi is, he has never been a student of higher education, this despite the timing of his past interactions with bitcoin.org[1].

- The lengths to which Satoshi went to disguise his identity have proved impossible to thwart, despite over a decade of intense investigations. This suggests a level of cybersecurity awareness comparable to employees of three-letter agencies, like the NSA or CIA.

- On the official profile for Satoshi Nakamoto on the Peer-to-Peer Foundation website, Satoshi lists his birthday as April 5, 1975, and his country of residence as Japan.

- Several programming experts familiar with Bitcoin say that Bitcoin's coding is simply too perfect to be the work of a single individual. More likely, they argue, Bitcoin was originally the result of a team collaborating for several months or even years before Nakamoto made the decision to present the code publicly.

In short, every time one finds a breadcrumb pointing to the real identity of Satoshi Nakamoto, it inevitably leads down one of several different rabbit holes.

Was Satoshi the Icelandic student genius Martti Malmi? Did Satoshi ever study at university? Was Satoshi British or just pretending to be British? Might Satoshi be Adam Back? Or was Satoshi always the Swiss privacy-focused tech mogul and early E-Gold adopter, Michael Niklaus Weber?

Frustratingly, it eventually becomes clear that every breadcrumb we think might unravel the mystery of Satoshi's identity has been

---

1. http://bitcoin.org

intentionally placed. This means that Satoshi didn't post on bitcoin.org during the same times a student might. Rather, he posted when he did so to purposefully appear as a student.

Likewise, Satoshi didn't share the same spelling and grammar as people like Weber. Neither did he really have a habit of leaving political Easter eggs in code like Adam Back. (After all, he only left one.) Satoshi was simply mimicking these people's known behaviors, knowing that doing so would better obfuscate his identity later.

Of course, Satoshi Nakamoto must have had prior knowledge of such people's behaviors in order to mimic them in the first place, and this would be entirely possible if Satoshi was always just a persona created by the likes of DARPA or the NSA. More specifically, a persona created by a team of people with access to data from the likes of the previously discussed TIA database.

Tinker Tailor Soldier Spy

To tell a lie is one thing. However, to obfuscate the truth so completely in the so-called information age is nothing short of astonishing. This accomplishment itself suggests that Satoshi Nakamoto was never a mere mortal—or at least a real human individual.

Let us remember also, that Bitcoin is a technology which demands expertise in several disparate fields to create anew, single-handedly. Satoshi, therefore, wasn't just a cryptographer; he was an outstanding programmer, had expertise in computer science, distributed computing, peer-to-peer networks, game theory, human psychology, national and international monetary policy, law, economics...

And he just came out of nowhere, before going back to wherever he came from in the blink of an eye.

In effect, Satoshi birthed the most magical technological unicorn of the century. One which by now makes him just as rich as Bill Gates. And then he just disappears. This, and he presumably watches from the sidelines as several hundred thousand people adopt, copy, and piggyback his creation, and become obscenely wealthy in the process.

None of this makes any sense. That is unless Satoshi simply never existed in the first place. What makes more sense, when we look at how choreographed his attempts were to appear as different people like Adam Back and Michael Niklaus Weber, is the premise that Satoshi Nakamoto was always just a persona put together in the same way as a CIA, NSA, MI5, or Mossad shell company.

Imagine a Boot Stamping on a Human Face Forever

I am not alone in my supposition that Satoshi Nakamoto never existed. Neither am I alone in my supposition that the Bitcoin origin story is really the story of a branch of the CIA or NSA pretending to be a grassroots cyberpunk movement here to liberate humanity from the shackles of the current financial status quo. Recently, former Fox News host Tucker Carlson hit the headlines by presenting the very same supposition.

As for why an agency like the CIA or NSA might have given us the gift of cryptocurrency in the first place, the most obvious reason is that which I have already presented in The Crypto Con. Namely, that for several years, society has been repeatedly nudged to accept the idea of one day "Cashless Society." Specifically, an economy where physical cash is completely replaced with digital information.

Bitcoin, to put it simply, has always just been a clever way to slowly condition humanity to think of cryptocurrency as cool, not a looming totalitarian nightmare of total financial state surveillance and interference.

The UK Public Authorities Fraud, Error, and Recovery Bill – An Orwellian Taste of Where Crypto Is Going

The UK government's new Public Authorities Fraud, Error and Recovery Bill is the most terrifying piece of legislation since the UK government's recent move to decriminalize abortion until just moments before birth. Likely, though, you know absolutely nothing about either of these two sneaky new laws. This being the case, let me paint you a picture of what the Fraud, Error and Recovery Bill means for you.

Imagine the scene. The year is 2030. You've recently broken up with your partner, your finances are stretched thinner than someone on their third dose of Ozempic, and you're late for work. To make matters worse, your car won't start. There is nothing mechanically wrong with your car, though. Rather, a smart kill switch in your vehicle has been activated by the UK Department for Work and Pensions. Why? Because they suspect you of being a benefit fraudster. Oh, and your bank account is frozen too.

Big Brother Is Finally Having the Red Carpet Rolled Out

To call the Public Authorities (Fraud, Error and Recovery) Bill draconian or Orwellian is an understatement. Its basic goal is to prevent benefit and tax fraud. However, to do so, it allows the UK government to trample over any expectations you might have of anything like a right to financial privacy.

At any time, the new bill allows the UK government to request up to three months of statements from your bank without you knowing. This can be done without a court order. If government agents can then identify evidence of benefit overpayments or tax being due on any money or assets you own, they can issue a direct deduction order. This is where money will be taken from your account to reimburse the government accordingly.

If you happen to own a joint account, the government can use direct deduction orders to confiscate cash, even if your partner is the one the government suspects of wrongdoing. Better yet, if the government suspects you of owing them £1,000 or more, they can invalidate your driver's license, making it impossible for you to drive. On this note, it's probably just a coincidence that all car manufacturers in the U.S. in 2026 (and soon in Europe too) will be mandated to include kill switches in all new car engines, which governments can use to disable vehicles remotely.

What the Public Authorities (Fraud, Error and Recovery) Bill Means for You

What the Public Authorities (Fraud, Error and Recovery) Bill means for the average British resident is simple: You should be afraid, very afraid.

On paper, you might work as a barista in a local coffee shop, earning minimum wage. As such, you might be eligible for some form of benefit or tax credit. What happens, though, when the DWP takes a look at your past three months of bank statements, only to see that you've been depositing cash from tips into your savings account? Or what if you've recently done a spring clean that saw you sell a bunch of things you no longer need on eBay?

In the eyes of the government, you aren't declaring all your income. Let's remember also that with access to your bank statements, the UK Department for Work and Pensions (DWP) can see exactly what you are spending your money on each month. This being the case, are you being more frivolous with your cash than the government might expect the average single mother to be? Might you, therefore, have some other undeclared income or financial assistance which might warrant further investigation?

Like It or Not, You're Guilty Until Proven Innocent

What is most striking about the Public Authorities Fraud, Error and Recovery Bill is that direct deductions will be taken from UK bank accounts the UK government suspects of holding fraudulently acquired funds, before account holders are able to question or petition such orders. This means that even if the DWP makes a mistake when secretly going over your bank statements, you will have to petition decisions after the government confiscates your cash.

Needless to say, fighting the UK government's decisions will be difficult if you can't hire a lawyer due to all your money already being in government coffers. It is also worth noting that you will have just 28 days to convince the government they have made a mistake. After 28 days, your money belongs to the state whether it was taken in error or not.

The Public Authorities Fraud, Error and Recovery Bill & The UK Post Office Horizon Scandal

Do you have nothing to hide? Are you a fine, upstanding Brit who can answer for every last penny of your current account balance? If so, that's fantastic. Let's remember, though, that governments themselves are far from savvy when it comes to accounting or keeping their own books in order.

Between 1999 and 2015, the UK Post Office prosecuted more than 900 postmasters (Post Office managers) in court for fraud after money was found routinely going missing from Post Office accounts.

Despite there being no proof, the Post Office and Crown Prosecution Service propagated the idea that there was a secret racket among Post Office managers where literally hundreds of postmasters every month were skimming funds from customer and company accounts.

Since 2015, at least four former Post Office postmasters have subsequently committed suicide, several have spent time in prison, and several more have been forced to cover Post Office losses out of their own pockets. There is just one problem: There was never any fraud. There wasn't even any money ever going missing.

After over twenty years of postmaster protests and independent investigations, it was finally revealed that all Post Office accounting irregularities were due to bugs in the Fujitsu accounting software the UK Post Office was using. Worse, postmasters working for the Post Office were warning of bugs in the software they were using from almost the day it came into use in 1999. None, though, have yet received compensation from the Post Office or UK government. However, Fujitsu to this day still regularly bids on new UK government contracts.

What Has Any of This Got to Do with Cryptocurrency?

When Bitcoin made its debut on the financial scene in 2009, early proponents of the cryptocurrency were quick to celebrate it as an answer to government overreaches. After all, if you use Bitcoin, no one can ever freeze your account/Bitcoin wallet funds. Nor can governments ever use anything like direct deduction orders to confiscate some or all of your wallet balance. There is just one problem.

As I have discussed extensively now in The Crypto Con, several central banks like the Bank of England, European Central Bank, and Bank for International Settlements in Switzerland (the central bank of central banks) all plan to soon start rolling out Central Bank Digital Currencies (CBDCs). The UK's Public Authorities Fraud, Error and Recovery Bill would also seem to be tailored more to the coming CBDC era than it is to the current cash era.

Today, governments have no way of knowing whether extra cash being deposited in your bank account is the result of a lucky win on a lottery scratch card, a gift from Grandma, or an undeclared cash-in-hand side hustle. This being the case, the Fraud, Error and Recovery Bill and similar legislation sneaking through governments worldwide is effectively impossible to implement. However, in a cashless future where every cent is programmable and instantly traceable to source, implementing such legislation will be much easier—especially with the help of AI.

Of course, one last hurdle to full implementation of such legislation is legacy cryptocurrency like Bitcoin. The only question is: Will the controllers of our looming cashless future allow legacy cryptocurrencies to exist in tandem with the CBDC era? Or are cryptocurrencies like Bitcoin soon set to be obliterated—and if so, how?

Threats to the Future Survival of Legacy Cryptocurrencies

In The Crypto Con, I refer to cryptocurrencies like Bitcoin as legacy cryptocurrencies. I do this to make a clear distinction between the cryptocurrencies which people are familiar with today, and Central Bank Digital Currencies currently being trialed by central banks, which are planned to start rolling out between now and 2030.

Whereas the vast majority of legacy cryptocurrencies are decentralized and not under the control of banks, governments, or private enterprises, CBDCs will be fully centralized and actively governed by such entities. There are also distinct technological differences between CBDCs and legacy cryptocurrencies. One of the most important of these concerns how both forms of cryptocurrency differ in terms of scalability, updateability, and basic security.

Consensus Vs Convenience

All forms of cryptocurrency are essentially just software applications. Both legacy cryptocurrencies and CBDCs subsequently require updating from time to time to add new features and patch newly discovered security vulnerabilities.

In the case of CBDCs, patching and updating cryptocurrencies is altogether easy. CBDC core software exists on central bank servers and databases which can be updated as soon as patches, updates, and security fixes are ready. However, with legacy cryptocurrencies like Bitcoin, things get a little more complicated.

The core software of legacy cryptocurrencies like Bitcoin is decentralized and distributed among millions of computers worldwide. Any updates are also only implemented when consensus is reached by at least 51% of the Bitcoin network that updates are valid and ultimately necessary. If consensus is not reached, updates either aren't applied, or the Bitcoin network splits, resulting in the formation of one or more new Bitcoin variants.

Bitcoin's 2018 Identity Crisis

The last time there was major lack of consensus when updating Bitcoin was in 2018. At the time, several developers and groups of Bitcoin miners were frustrated with the 2MB limit on Bitcoin transaction block sizes. It was widely known that this 2MB limit was always intended by Satoshi Nakamoto himself to be temporary. It was, therefore, argued that this limit should be lifted in order to significantly increase Bitcoin transaction speeds.

On the other side of the update fence, several other Bitcoin developers and miners held the view that Bitcoin should stay as it was. While Satoshi's limiting of transaction block sizes was always intended to be temporary, they argued that slower transaction speeds make Bitcoin more of a long-term investment vehicle like gold. Increase block sizes to allow transactions to settle instantly, and Bitcoin might just become like any other 2018 altcoin competing for the crown of the fastest coin in town.

As no consensus could be reached, the Bitcoin network split in two. The original Bitcoin with its 2MB block size continued to function. However, a new Bitcoin with a much larger 32MB transaction block size was created. This coin still exists today in the form of Bitcoin Cash. However, further disputes would see the Bitcoin Cash network later split again to create a new Bitcoin variant with an eye-popping 128MB block size called Bitcoin SV.

If this wasn't confusing enough for investors, all three Bitcoin variants insisted that they were the one and only true Bitcoin. Thankfully, most investors at the time chose to remain loyal to the original Bitcoin being maintained by one of the original Bitcoin.org members Adam Back, and his team at Blockstream. However, this episode still stands to prove how major updates to legacy cryptocurrencies using distributed ledger technology can be problematic.

Legacy Cryptocurrencies and The Quantum Computing Time Bomb

As I have stated previously, the cybersecurity landscape in which Bitcoin originally rose to prominence couldn't be more different to the cybersecurity landscape of the present day. However, it is not just backdoor subsystems in all modern Intel computers which legacy crypto developers and maintainers need to take heed of.

When Satoshi Nakamoto authored the original Bitcoin white paper, things like quantum computing were still largely theoretical concepts. Fast forward to today, and quantum computers aren't just part of our computing reality already. As well as quantum computers, we also have increasingly sophisticated artificial intelligence technologies being used in increasingly sophisticated cyber attacks. The time for legacy cryptocurrencies like Bitcoin and Ethereum to become hardened against such threats was, therefore, yesterday. However, they still haven't been.

Bitcoin Needs to Go Down for 76 Days - Or Stagger Transactions for 10 Months

Because Central Bank Digital Currencies are still in active research and development, we can be fairly certain that by the time they arrive they will already be resilient to known quantum computing attack vectors. As new threats manifest, central banks will also be able to update and patch CBDCs in real time.

By comparison, researchers at the University of Kent's School of Computing predict that to become quantum computing resistant, Bitcoin itself will eventually need to go offline for a minimum of 76 days. During this period of downtime, all existing Bitcoin miners and network maintainers would need to commit to performing necessary upgrades. However, this will simply never happen.

If it is ever announced that Bitcoin is about to go offline for just a few days or even hours, investors will quickly panic-sell any Bitcoin they own and abandon the digital currency.

Mining farms mining Bitcoin also need to make a profit to survive. This being the case, they can't dedicate 76 days of resources to what is essentially a massive software update, (during which time they won't recoup basic operating costs). The minute Bitcoin becomes unprofitable to mine, miners will simply switch to mining cryptocurrencies which are still profitable. The resources to adequately harden Bitcoin against quantum computing threats, therefore, simply won't be there.

Thankfully, the same University of Kent School of Computing study suggests that Bitcoin might be able to devote just 25% of all network resources to performing necessary quantum computing resistance upgrades. However, this would see upgrades take a minimum of 305 days as opposed to just 76. This would also see Bitcoin transactions take 25% longer to process.

At the time of writing, there is no official roadmap detailing when or how Bitcoin will take any step to become hardened against future quantum computing threats. This in itself is a problem, as while some researchers believe that Bitcoin might still have 10 years to become quantum computing resistant, others point at the speed at which AI is evolving, and say that the best conservative estimates will see quantum computing pose a threat to Bitcoin in as few as three to four years.

The First Quantum Computing Threat to Bitcoin Appeared in 1994

If it will take almost a full year to future-proof Bitcoin against new quantum computing attack vectors, the time to do so was yesterday. This is especially true when we consider the fact that the first quantum computing threat to Bitcoin actually appeared in 1994.

Bitcoin and all cryptocurrencies based on the original Bitcoin codebase use asymmetric cryptography to secure wallets and transactions. This sees Bitcoin users use a private cryptographic key known only to them, which secures their Bitcoin wallet balance. A second public key visible to anyone subsequently acts as a Bitcoin address which funds can be sent and received by.

What most people are not aware of is the fact that a quantum computing algorithm capable of breaking asymmetric cryptography was devised way back in 1994 by the mathematician Peter Shor. All that has been lacking since 1994 is a powerful enough quantum computer to actually run the Shor algorithm.

Put as simply as possible, when we do have a quantum computer capable of running Shor's algorithm, it will be able to crack the private keys of individual Bitcoin users. At that point, a quantum computing user will be able to transact the funds belonging to whatever private key they crack as if those funds are their own.

In theory, quantum computers which are already in use like those made available by Canadian tech company D-Wave Systems are already capable of disrupting Bitcoin transaction processing. However, such systems are used chiefly for academic research. What researchers worry about when it comes to quantum computing is the day when such machines become more easily accessible to the general public and malicious nation states.

Bitcoin's Existential 51% Attack Vector

Quantum computing and faster update and scalability capabilities which will give future Central Bank Digital Currencies a security advantage over legacy cryptocurrencies aren't the only threats facing today's legacy cryptocurrencies.

In the case of Bitcoin, Satoshi Nakamoto himself warned us how Bitcoin will always be susceptible to a 51% attack. This is where Bitcoin miners might decide to unite, or a hacker might use a botnet to take control of over 51% of all computers maintaining the decentralized Bitcoin transaction ledger.

If a 51% attack were ever to be successful, whatever entity ends up controlling 51% of the Bitcoin network will instantly have the ability to start invalidating transactions, emptying wallets, and even start changing the basic protocols that govern how Bitcoin works. Neither would it matter if you hold your Bitcoin on a non-Internet-connected device like a cryptocurrency hardware wallet. If instigators of a 51% attack want your wallet balance, all they have to do is reverse the last transaction that saw you deposit your Bitcoin on your hardware wallet in the first place.

To many involved with cryptocurrency, the idea of a 51% attack being successful against a decentralized cryptocurrency like Bitcoin often seems absurd. However, as of summer 2025, successful 51% attacks on cryptocurrency networks have begun to take place in the wild.

In mid-2025, Qubic, a new AI-powered blockchain, used a novel strategy to stage a successful 51% attack against the privacy coin Monero.

Over a relatively short period, Qubic was successful in incentivizing miners of several other cryptocurrencies to switch to mining Monero. Eventually, this gave Qubic 51% control over the entire Monero network. Gaining 51% control of Monero subsequently gave Qubic the power to begin double-spending Monero wallet balances. (This is where the same Monero coins can be used twice when being traded for other currencies.)

Qubic could have also begun invalidating past, present, and future transactions, thereby invalidating the use of Monero completely. The only reason this didn't happen was because Qubic wasn't acting maliciously. As part of what is referred to as an "ethical hack," Qubic only gained 51% control over Monero to prove that such an attack was possible.

The Intel Inside or NSA Inside Problem

Now that Bitcoin is less truly decentralized than it has ever been, and now that we know that individual mining pools already have the ability to prevent transactions from settling, a 51% attack on Bitcoin in the way Satoshi Nakamoto warned us about is more likely than it has ever been. Such an attack could also conceivably happen in a way which completely blindsides cyber security experts and cryptocurrency blockchain maintainers.

As I've already discussed in The Crypto Con chapter: T*he Unspoken Vulnerability of EVERY Cryptocurrency,* hardware-based subsystems in all modern CPUs exist which are essentially the equivalent of having a second computer inside your computer. In the case of the Intel Management Engine, the IME even has its very own operating system called Minix, as well as its own independent network stack. Vulnerabilities to both the IME and Minix are also already out in the wild.

In theory, it will one day be possible for someone with full access to the IME (whether access is given or acquired by brute force) to create botnets which could disrupt the likes of the Bitcoin network by acquiring control of 51% or more computers contributing to Bitcoin transaction processing. Intel, after all, dominates approximately 70% of the consumer PC market, and nearly 80% of the commercial server market.

In effect, if the NSA or a similar three-letter agency ever wanted a Bitcoin kill switch, the IME is that kill switch.

Cryptocurrencies Coming Confidence Problem

It is not just Bitcoin which has to harden itself against quantum computing, AI, increasing centralization, and increasing hardware-based cyber security threats. Ethereum, every token on Ethereum, and almost every top trading cryptocurrency currently on the market share the same vulnerabilities. Neither are such vulnerabilities exaggerated or a matter of conjecture.

Thanks to people like IBM Quantum's Jay Gambetta and a June 2025 U.S. House Committee hearing: "Preparing for the Quantum Age: When Cryptography Breaks," it is a known fact that several nation states are currently harvesting encrypted data and cryptocurrency public keys, in anticipation of having future quantum decryption capabilities. This, though, begs the question: Why isn't Bitcoin quantum ready already?

To put this question in perspective, alternative cryptocurrency projects like Cardano have been embedding quantum computing resistance into their blockchains since 2016. Quantum computing isn't, therefore, a new challenge for Bitcoin that has suddenly sprung up out of nowhere. Rather, it's been staring Bitcoin down the barrel of a gun for over a decade, and Bitcoin has just stared back like a rabbit paralyzed by a pair of headlights.

There is no solution in sight. There is no action plan. There is no attempt to even address the threat in question.

If Bitcoin was a bank, this inaction wouldn't exactly inspire investor or customer confidence. Neither would the fact that crucial security updates to basic bank security infrastructure might take up to a year—if such updates are ever agreed upon at all. This in itself poses another problem for today's legacy cryptocurrency market.

Central bank digital currencies are coming. When they arrive, they will already be hardened against the cyber security threats we are now discussing. Should new threats emerge on the cyber security scene, they will also update and harden themselves in a matter of minutes or hours, not months or days like legacy cryptocurrencies. Where, therefore, would you choose to hold your money?

If CBDCs do arrive on schedule around 2030, they will possibly arrive in tandem with the first real quantum computing challenges to legacy cryptocurrencies. Moreover, just one successful attack on either Bitcoin or Ethereum would see investor confidence in legacy cryptocurrency evaporate overnight. This might even be why market-leading coins like

Bitcoin have been suspiciously slow to harden themselves against such challenges.

We have a wealth of circumstantial evidence to suggest that Bitcoin might not only have been created by the NSA, but might have also been protected by the same agency as the early cryptocurrency market was gaining momentum. Might it, therefore, be possible that the same powers might now be nudging Bitcoin toward a planned obsolescence of sorts?

Is Bitcoin a Bubble?

What if I told you that right now the value of Bitcoin represents the biggest bubble in financial history? Worse, what if I were to tell you that when the current Bitcoin bubble bursts, the cataclysmic financial aftermath will affect you directly, even if you have never bought Bitcoin or invested in the cryptocurrency market?

What if I were to also tell you that governments, central banks, and financial regulators all around the world have been aware of this bubble for at least the past eight years? This, and that the very same agencies are waiting for the current crypto bubble to burst with giddy expectation?

I won't leave you in suspense any longer. If there is one simple reason why no one in 2025 should invest in Bitcoin or other cryptocurrency, its name is Tether.

Bitcoin & Tether – A Match Made in Financial Armageddon

As I have already made clear in The Crypto Con, the value of Bitcoin is based entirely on belief. If a significant number of people believe Bitcoin has value, it has value. By comparison, if belief ever falters, so do Bitcoin market prices. This is why the market prices of Bitcoin and other cryptocurrencies can fluctuate wildly on exchanges.

If you are someone who trades cryptocurrency professionally, such price swings can be catastrophic. After all, even the best traders can't predict which way markets are about to move with 100% accuracy.

Thankfully, though, they don't have to. This is because in 2014, something called stablecoins were invented.

What Are Stablecoins?

Stablecoins are cryptocurrencies. However, stablecoins differ from coins like Bitcoin in that they have a 1-to-1 redeemability against real currencies like the U.S. dollar. The most famous of these is the stablecoin Tether. Moreover, how stablecoins help traders profit more when trading cryptocurrency is simple.

Almost all cryptocurrency exchanges where people trade cryptocurrencies support Bitcoin and Tether trading pairs. This means that Bitcoin traders can instantly exchange Bitcoin for an equivalent amount of Tether whenever they like.

To put this simply, let's say you own $100,000 worth of Bitcoin. If you think the Bitcoin price might soon start to go down, you can instantly exchange the $100,000 worth of Bitcoin you own for $100,000 worth of the stablecoin Tether.

Because Tether is backed on a 1-to-1 basis by the USD, you will still have $100,000 even if the price of Bitcoin falls to zero overnight. Even better, if you think that the price of Bitcoin will recover, you can use your $100,000 in Tether (USDT) to buy back your Bitcoin at a lower price. If the Bitcoin price subsequently recovers, you will end up with a greater amount of Bitcoin with a higher equivalent dollar value than you had before.

Why Use Tether and Other Stablecoins to Do This?

Why people use stablecoins to trade Bitcoin this way is simple. It is possible to trade Bitcoin for regular cash on exchanges. However, real-world banks and credit card issuers often limit the amount of cash users can trade with. Bank fees and transaction processing times also make it impossible for people to trade Bitcoin for regular cash instantly. This is why traders choose to use stablecoins.

At present, there are several stablecoins on the cryptocurrency market. However, Tether (USDT) was the very first on the scene. Tether is also one of the most widely accepted on exchanges and is subsequently the go-to stablecoin for most cryptocurrency traders.

The Trouble With Tether

Tether may be the most popular stablecoin on the cryptocurrency market. However, mounting evidence suggests that Tether might not actually hold enough real U.S. dollars in reserve to genuinely be backed on a 1-to-1 basis by the U.S. dollar itself. Many people also believe that Tether Limited, the company that controls Tether, regularly creates millions of dollars' worth of unbacked USDT coins to artificially inflate the price of Bitcoin.

If these allegations are true, this would mean that Bitcoin and Tether work in tandem to make Bitcoin itself nothing more than the world's biggest ever Ponzi scheme.

Mounting Evidence Suggests That Tether Is NOT a Stablecoin

For a stablecoin to be a true stablecoin, it is of paramount importance that every single coin has the genuine backing of a real U.S. dollar. In a worst-case scenario, after all, Bitcoin might one day go to zero. If this happens and you were smart enough to exchange all your Bitcoin for Tether beforehand, you will, therefore, still expect to be able to exchange all your Tether for real U.S. dollars and not lose a dime. This is the whole point of using Tether in the first place.

Sadly, there has been a whirlwind of controversy surrounding Tether since at least 2017. This is due to the fact that no one has ever been permitted to independently audit Tether's accounts. No one can, therefore, independently verify that every USDT (U.S. Dollar Tether) currently in circulation has the backing of a real U.S. dollar as Tether claims. It might even be the case that Tether has never been backed on a 1-to-1 basis by real U.S. dollar reserves.

In 2021, the New York Attorney General slapped Tether and its parent company iFinex Inc. with an $18.5 million fine. Why? Because it was found that Tether and the iFinex-owned cryptocurrency exchange Bitfinex had mixed client and corporate funds to cover an $85 million black hole in their combined finances.

Later in 2022, the U.S. Commodity Futures Trading Commission (CFTC) hit Tether Limited with an even bigger $42.5 million fine for lying about their reserves. In fact, what the CFTC found was that between 2016 and 2018, Tether was only 26% backed by real U.S. dollars. This despite swearing otherwise.

Since these rulings, Tether has started stating that it backs every USDT coin it creates with real U.S. dollars and what Tether calls "cash equivalents." Currently, these cash equivalents include land purchases, other cryptocurrencies (including Bitcoin), and U.S. Treasury bonds. In fact, at present, Tether owns more U.S. Treasury bonds than whole countries like Germany and South Korea. However, Tether still won't let anyone independently audit their books. Neither does controversy surrounding Tether end here.

The now convicted fraudster Sam Bankman-Fried used Tether as the go-to stablecoin on his own cryptocurrency exchange, FTX. The parent company of FTX, Alameda Research, also partnered with Tether and itself minted $39.55 billion Tether coins, which is over a quarter of all Tether still in circulation today. It has also since been proven that Alameda Research didn't have reserves to cover the amount of Tether it was minting. However, this didn't stop Alameda Research from routinely redeeming billions of Tether for real U.S. dollars as it was minting the stablecoin at the same time. Alameda Research was, if you like, really just printing digital money out of thin air before exchanging this as it did so for real cash.

Why Is It a Problem If Tether Isn't Backed on a 1-to-1 Basis with Real U.S. Dollars?

Why Tether coins not being backed on a 1-to-1 basis by real U.S. dollars is a problem is simple. Firstly, if you hold funds in Tether, there may come a day when it will not be possible to exchange the Tether you own for real cash or equivalents of other cryptocurrencies.

Think about this. Between 2016 and 2018, Tether swore that every USDT coin was backed by a real U.S. dollar. However, it has since been proven that Tether only had enough cash reserves to back 26% of all USDT coins then in circulation. This means that if you bought Tether during this time, you were effectively trading $1 for something with a real-world value of just 26 cents.

It is also important to keep in mind that between 2015 and 2018, Bitcoin rose from $500 in value to a peak of over $20,000. However, as a 2018 paper titled "Is Bitcoin Really Un-Tethered?" by researchers John M. Griffin and Amin Shams alleges, the Bitcoin price during Bitcoin's rise to $20,000 in 2017 was driven predominantly by "one entity," namely, Tether. If this is true, it means that Bitcoin's true value when it hit $20,000 should have been something around $5,200.

How Can Tether Possibly Be Responsible for Inflating Cryptocurrency Prices?

If Tether is not backed on a 1-to-1 basis, anyone who ever buys Tether risks losing some or all of their funds if too many people try to exchange Tether they own for real U.S. dollars at once. It also means that the current price of Bitcoin is far higher than it should be. The only question is, how could Tether possibly be inflating the price of Bitcoin?

At present, Tether Limited says that it only creates new Tether (USDT) coins to meet consumer demand. This being the case, when cryptocurrency traders and investors see Tether creating millions of dollars' worth of new USDT coins before sending coins to exchanges, they assume that there is increasing demand for Bitcoin itself. Investors, especially new-to-market investors, subsequently rush to buy Bitcoin.

As noted in research by the Journal of Finance, there is also evidence that when Tether today creates new USDT coins and sends them to exchanges to meet alleged demand, cryptocurrency exchanges themselves then distribute this Tether to smaller, subsidiary exchanges, which almost always sees the price of Bitcoin begin to climb within a few hours.

If you are someone who isn't involved in the cryptocurrency space, some of the above may already be a little difficult to understand. However, all should become clear when we take a look at just how much Tether (USDT) creates each month and deposits on exchanges.

As verified by the cryptocurrency exchange Binance, Tether created and sent the following amount of new Tether coins to exchanges in just the first 5 months of 2025:

- January 2025 – 1 billion USDT

- February 2025 – 3 billion US
- March 2025 – 4 billion USDT
- 2025 – 6 billion USDT
- May 2025 – 6 billion USDT

Now remember, all Tether coins are supposedly backed on a 1-to-1 basis by real U.S. dollars or cash equivalents. This means that on top of the reserves Tether had in December 2024, Tether was able to find $1 billion to create 1 billion new Tether coins to deposit on exchanges the following January. Then in February, Tether Limited was able to fund another round of Tether printing to the tune of $3 billion?

Can you name a company that can raise a billion or three billion of investment funds each month? Can you name one which has $3 billion or $6 billion in ready cash or profits each month which it can afford to invest back into itself? The simple answer is probably not.

Now let's take a look at the total amount of Tether created in 2024:

- December 2024 – 5 billion USDT
- November 2024 – 13 billion USDT
- 2024 – 1 billion USD
- September 2024 – 1 billion USDT
- August 2024 – 3 billion USDT
- July 2024 – 1 billion USDT
- June 2024 – 1 billion USDT

- May 2024 – 2 billion USDT
- April 2024 – 5 billion USDT
- March 2024 – 6 billion USDT
- February 2024 – 2 billion USDT
- January 2024 – 5 billion USDT

Yes, the total amount of Tether created by Tether Limited in 2024 was over $45 billion. Moreover, Tether has been creating and making available new Tether coins at this scale since 2016, with the majority of USDT (Tether) created being used to buy Bitcoin.

It doesn't take a genius to see that there is something very wrong here. This is especially true when we consider the fact that Tether, despite supposedly being a company with more cash than Apple, refuses to allow anyone to audit its accounts.

The Great Big Imaginary Money Game

The way Tether Limited operates has been likened by some to how central banks operate. Tether creates its own currency out of thin air, of which only a small percentage is ever backed by real assets. Unbacked USDT is then used to buy Bitcoin, which pushes the price of Bitcoin higher and higher. Tether also gets away with this by operating offshore, far from the reach of financial regulators.

Eventually, the rug will get pulled. Moreover, when confidence in Tether fails, it will fail fast. The mass realization that for nearly a decade, the Bitcoin price has been pushed higher by billions of dollars of Tether monopoly money, will also result in a catastrophic devaluing of assets like Bitcoin and other top market cap cryptocurrencies.

None of this is speculation. The only question on the mind cryptocurrency insiders whom are aware of how Tether operates is when, not if Tether's game will ever finally be rumbled.

The NSA Key – The 1999 NSA Backdoor Into Windows

In The Crypto Con, I've repeatedly asserted that the use case and integrity of Bitcoin—and all forms of cryptocurrency—have been compromised right from the beginning. This is due to the existence of hardware backdoors in all of the hardware we use to buy, sell, and store cryptocurrency.

As I have already taken pains to make clear, every modern Intel, ARM, and AMD CPU on the market has a dedicated subsystem. These subsystems are best described in simple terms as discrete secondary CPUs embedded inside the known central processors that form the heart of modern computers and smart devices.

In some cases, these subsystems have their own networking capabilities. This means they can communicate via Bluetooth, Wi-Fi, and sometimes cellular networks, even when your device is powered off. (And even if you use physical hardware controls on your device to disable things like Wi-Fi and Bluetooth.)

In every case, these subsystems also have privileged access to your physical device data storage area, device operating system, and any software your device runs.

What this means from a cybersecurity standpoint is simple. As a device user, you have no access or control over the chip inside the CPU of your device. In fact, if you ever try to access or disable such a subsystem, you will likely brick your device, making it incapable of ever booting again. However, bad actors like hackers and three-letter agencies like the CIA may have access. In fact, such actors could be perusing all your most sensitive data—including any cryptocurrency you own right now—and you would never have any way of knowing.

Of course, Intel, AMD, and ARM all argue that the presence of such subsystems is wholly benevolent. In business contexts, the likes of Intel's Management Engine allows business users to remotely manage systems even when systems are powered off or suspected of being stolen. However, this doesn't explain why everyday computer users can't disable such systems, especially given the fact that hackers have already compromised the security of such subsystems previously. You can't even turn this so-called security feature off, even on stripped-down devices intended for use as toys for small children. The looming question is, subsequently, why not?

Naturally, Intel and other CPU vendors are quick to malign any talk of such subsystems being backdoors into personal computers as nothing more than conspiracy. However, there is evidence that agencies like America's National Security Agency (NSA) have had direct backdoors into at least all Windows computers since the mid-1990s.

What Is the NSA Key?

Until the release of Windows XP in 2001, a Windows software driver file labeled "ADVAPI.dll" had long represented something of an enigma to cybersecurity specialists. It was known that the driver was responsible for a range of encryption tasks in Windows. However, ADVAPI.dll seemed to have some unusual and intentionally obscured features present in every iteration of the .dll file from Windows 95 onward. Then, in 1999, researchers began to realize why certain features might be obscured.

When Windows makes updates available to current operating systems, it does so in the form of stripped binary files. To make this simple to understand, when Windows developers are coding updates, they include a lot of information intended for human use. A developer may, for example, isolate a section of code and label it as something like "New Skin for Windows Media Player."

When developers do this, they are making it easier for other developers to know what specific pieces of code in what can be large update files addressing several issues at once actually do. This makes it easy for other developers to double-check and debug code before it is released. However, adding identifiers (or what are known as debugging symbols) to code like this also makes the overall size of Windows Update files much larger.

To make update files smaller, software vendors like Microsoft strip code of debugging symbols before updates go live. This makes downloads faster and makes proprietary code more secure, as it is difficult for anyone who might intercept files to take raw data and identify what individual bits of code actually do. However, on May 4, 1999, Windows accidentally released an update to all NT4-generation Windows operating systems without first stripping the final update file of its debugging symbols.

One of the first cybersecurity researchers to realize Microsoft's mistake was British computer scientist Nicko van Someren. What Someren found sent shockwaves through the 1999 cybersecurity scene. This was because, pertaining directly to Microsoft's ADVAPI.dll driver file, Someren found two cryptographic keys. One labeled as "Key," and the other ominously labeled "NSAKey."

Both of these keys were cryptographic public keys. This means that they would be used by the host Windows operating system to verify the integrity of new software signed by a trusted software vendor's private key.

To make this simple, think of BitLocker encryption that Windows uses today. You can use your system login and password to access BitLocker and encrypt or decrypt your data. You can also generate a recovery phrase to use should you ever get locked out of BitLocker. However, only Microsoft has the private key to the BitLocker software you are using. All you have is the public key that allows your computer to verify that Microsoft's version of BitLocker your computer is communicating with is genuine.

Given the above, the existence of a Microsoft public key in a Windows update file isn't unusual. With such a key, a computer can verify that software and updates from Windows and other trusted software vendors are genuine. The presence of an NSA key, though, would imply that the National Security Agency of the United States could also push programs and updates to Windows (likely without users knowing), which would also be acknowledged by Windows as legitimate and be installed accordingly.

To put this in perspective, hackers love simple programs like keyloggers. These are programs that secretly record every key you press on your keyboard and send this data back to malicious third parties. Such parties then have access to anything you might have typed while using your computer. This can include anything from the contents of sensitive emails to website addresses, user login details, and user passwords for everything from online banking apps to secure online databases.

Thankfully, malicious third parties can only install things like keylogging apps on user devices if they have direct access to devices or can trick device users into installing apps themselves. However, if the NSA Key found in Windows in 1999 is genuine, this would mean that the NSA could discreetly push malicious programs like keyloggers to individual computers (or whole networks of computers), which would then be authorized to run by Windows itself.

All of this is, of course, only possible if the NSA key is/was really a key pertaining to the National Security Agency. To this day, Microsoft denies this. However, Microsoft took two official stances when rebuking its existence. Firstly, Microsoft argued that the discovered key was simply a misnamed genuine Windows backup key. At the same time, though, Microsoft made it clear that United States export rules exist which forbid Microsoft (and other technology vendors) from exporting encryption technologies overseas that the NSA is incapable of deciphering.

In a way, Microsoft was saying, "Don't worry, there's nothing to see here," but by the way, the NSA has access to your operating system anyway. It has to; that's the law.

This, in itself, is alarming, as this would imply that the NSA key found in Windows was not just genuine, but also part of a much larger NSA strategy to ensure that the agency was able to compromise the encryption of all 1990s consumer technologies.

No doubt, this will seem far-fetched to some. However, at the same time that the so-called NSA key was discovered in Windows, it was also revealed that in 1997, Lotus—a Microsoft Office competitor—had been forced by the NSA to weaken its own encryption. Namely, so as to give the NSA a backdoor into all documents and emails created using the Lotus Notes Office Suite, used by millions of individuals, businesses, and governments worldwide. Keep in mind that this is also a recorded fact, not speculation or hearsay.

Other Known NSA Backdoors & Security Agency Cybersecurity Threats

For the most part, when average consumers with only a passing understanding of cybersecurity think of cybersecurity threats, they bring to mind wholly software-based threats. However, thanks to people like Edward Snowden, we know that since at least the mid-2000s, agencies like the NSA have strived to embed physical security backdoors into most of the must-have consumer technologies we rely on to live our digital lives through.

Within the thousands of classified NSA documents that Edward Snowden released in May 2013, there are details of an NSA program implemented by the Signals Intelligence arm of the NSA (SIGINT), the aim of which was, by 2013, to have embedded backdoors into a wide range of new-to-market microprocessors specializing in encryption.

Embedded subsystems on laptop and desktop CPUs—like the Intel Management Engine and AMD's Platform Security Processor—would certainly seem to fit the bill when it comes to the aim of the SIGINT program. However, it's not just hidden microcontrollers in modern computer CPUs that we need to worry about.

Few in the IT sector will ever forget the release of Windows 8.0 in 2012. This was the successor to Windows 7, which famously dispensed with the traditional Windows Start Menu. Instead, Windows users who upgraded to Windows 8 were met with Windows' new "Metro" desktop metaphor.

While a delight for some touchscreen device users, the new so-called "Start Screen" caused nothing but headaches for businesses and Windows power users. However, in Germany, it wasn't just the change in the standard user interface of Windows that upset some cybersecurity researchers.

On the coattails of Windows 8.0 in 2012 came a new generation of computers equipped with Trusted Platform Module (TPM) chips. Their purpose? Officially, TPM-equipped devices and their successors today are used to harden host operating systems against security threats like malware and viruses. They do this by working with host operating systems to determine what software can and cannot be installed on a device, and they do this completely independently of device users.

Let's say that you accidentally download an inauthentic version of Microsoft Office. Thanks to the way Microsoft securely signs its software and the way TPM chips work, the TPM chip in your computer will prevent your computer from running the software you have downloaded. TPM technology also makes it impossible to run so-called cracked versions of Windows and, in theory, malware like keylogging programs, which we discussed earlier.

Preventing known malware from running on Windows computers sounds at first like an indisputably good thing. However, in Germany, the Federal Office for Information Security quickly raised alarm over TPM and Windows 8. This was due to the fact that Trusted Platform Module security chips and compatible computer operating systems completely remove control from end computer users over what software is allowed or not allowed to run on TPM-enabled hardware. In fact, the problem with TPM is similar to that posed by the so-called NSA key from way back in 1999.

While the Trusted Platform Module chip in most contemporary computer motherboards can prevent malicious third parties from booting alternative operating systems or malicious software, the TPM chip only does what its programmers want, not what end computer users might want. If the likes of the NSA (who are leading promoters of

TPM technology) therefore have access to chips during manufacture, they can essentially decide which of their own programs are allowed to run on devices, without end device users ever knowing.

Ultimately, TPM and associated secure boot technologies could even one day be used to prevent computer users from running non-Microsoft operating systems like Linux, and/or only applications from official Microsoft, Apple, and Android app stores.

This was why German authorities urged state departments to avoid using Windows 8 on launch. Moreover, this is why several German and European powers have since begun migrating from Windows to open-source operating systems like Linux.

As one internal document from Germany's Ministry of Economic Affairs in 2012 states:

"Due to the loss of full sovereignty over information technology, the security goals of 'confidentiality' and 'integrity' are no longer guaranteed." The same document goes on to state: "This could have significant impacts on the IT security of the Federal Administration," before concluding by saying that: "The use of 'Trusted Computing' technology in this form... is unacceptable for the Federal Administration and for the operators of critical infrastructure."

In short, German IT officials strongly suspected that the likes of the NSA really did have access to the Trusted Platform Module chips in new Windows computers.

Rüdiger Weis, a professor at Beuth University of Applied Sciences in Berlin, also went as far as to identify three theoretical ways in which TPM chips could be vulnerable not just to NSA spying, but also to spying by Chinese intelligence services (due to the fact that all TPM chips are manufactured in China).

The Enigma Enigma You Probably Don't Know About

Were German state officials in 2012 just being paranoid about the idea of the NSA—and possibly the Chinese—having a backdoor into all new Windows 8 computers? In short, probably not. It was Germany, after all, that set the stage for the modern age of encryption and cybersecurity as we know it.

From the 1920s until near the end of WWII, Germany was leagues ahead of the rest of the world when it came to its military and government communicating via state-of-the-art encryption. We're talking, of course, about Enigma.

Originally, Enigma machines were commercially available electromechanical ciphers available to German domestic as well as military users. They worked by using rotors that swapped pairs of letters on a keyboard to encrypt messages that could be sent via telegram. Every day, the settings of linked pairs of Enigma machines would be changed so that even if a cipher sent by Enigma was broken once, ciphers the next day would remain secure.

Secured exclusively for military use during WWII, the use of Enigma gave Germany a significant edge over Allied forces. This was why the British famously enlisted the visionary mathematician Alan Turing to head a special group at Bletchley Park tasked with breaking the Enigma code. Today, we know that this effort was successful. However, what most people in the West aren't aware of is the fact that the United Kingdom and the United States kept the breaking of Enigma a shared state secret until long after WWII was over.

Why breaking Enigma was kept secret was simple. When the Second World War was over, the U.S. and UK went to lengths to gift fellow allies captured Enigma machines which they could use to send and receive secure interstate communications and diplomatic cables. All that allies of the UK and U.S. weren't aware of for several years post-WWII was the fact that the Enigma code had long been broken and that, as a result, the UK and U.S. had gifted Enigma machines only to spy themselves on all their correspondence.

Global Military-Grade Encryption Backdoors

Following on from the success of using German Enigma machines to snoop on allies long after WWII, the CIA went one step further in the 1970s by secretly purchasing a Swiss company called Crypto AG. At the time, Crypto AG specialized in the manufacturing of next-level military-grade encrypted communications technology.

The goal of acquiring Crypto AG was simple. Switzerland, as a country, has a habit of abstaining from most global conflicts. Granted, Swiss banks have a habit of offering their financial services to both sides of many such conflicts. However, for the most part, Switzerland is perceived as a neutral political power on the world stage. The CIA, therefore, hoped that by secretly acquiring Crypto AG, they could dominate the world of secure, encrypted communications by building clandestine backdoors into all Crypto AG technologies.

Fast forward to the mid-1990s, and Crypto AG was regularly selling supposedly state-of-the-art encryption and cipher technologies to over 120 countries, including Libya, Iran, India, Pakistan, and several countries in South America. All that Crypto AG customers were not aware of was the fact that backdoors existed in all such devices, which gave the United States, UK, and Germany clandestine access to even the most secure and sensitive of communications.

It was only in 2018 that the CIA's Crypto AG racket was rumbled.

Over the same period, the American-owned military-grade microchip manufacturer Actel was busy building backdoors into a host of chips used in defense technologies and critical civil infrastructure systems, even those tasked with securing the safety of international nuclear power plants and nuclear material transport systems. Some even argue that such Actel backdoors form the basis of how nuclear- and critical infrastructure-specific cybersecurity threats like Stuxnet are able to be deployed and compromise foreign civil and defense infrastructure platforms so absolutely.

Going Postal

Given the fact that for over half a century, the United States intelligence services have gone to several extraordinary lengths to backdoor almost all global encrypted communications, the idea that the same intelligence services might have a backdoor into your home computer shouldn't seem so shocking.

Let's also remember that the 1997 backdoor into the Lotus Notes Office Suite isn't a matter of conjecture. This backdoor did exist, was exposed, and was used by the NSA to spy on Lotus Office Suite-created documents and emails.

At the same time, Lotus regularly gave away free versions of its software in the form of free demo CDs in popular computing magazines. It is, therefore, not the case that the NSA was hoping to gather data from a few niche people of interest. Rather, they knew full well that most people using Lotus were regular, often budget-conscious home computer users. Why then would the likes of the NSA not have a similar way of infiltrating Windows today?

When thinking about this, we should also keep in mind that agencies like the NSA mandate that all microprocessor subsystems—like the Intel Management Engine embedded in all current consumer technologies—are disabled before devices become part of government or NSA agency networks. They still insist that these subsystems are safe and definitely not backdoors. They just don't want them inside their own computers.

Thankfully, there are computer vendors like System76 who allow regular members of the public to purchase modern computers with subsystems like the Intel Management Engine disabled. It is also theoretically possible to avoid security risks posed by the likes of the Intel Management Engine by simply using older, pre-2008 computer hardware. There is just one problem.

According to the NSA whistleblower Edward Snowden, the NSA operates a department called the NSA Access and Target Development Department. This is an entire department tasked with using the postal service to intercept computer and networking technologies ordered online.

On being intercepted, packages are opened, inspected, and contents are implanted with hardware backdoors (if they don't have them already) before being forwarded on to unsuspecting consumers.

Of course, there is the old saying that if you have nothing to hide, you have nothing to fear. However, if you are purposefully looking for the likes of a System76 computer to avoid being (potentially) spied on by government agencies, this would imply that you have something to hide.

It should also be kept in mind that three-letter agencies like the NSA don't spy on individuals or groups retroactively after flagging individuals or groups as security threats. Rather, and as previously discussed, such agencies strive to have constant, real-time, total information awareness (TIA).

Put simply, you are not a person of interest. Everyone, everywhere, all the time is a person of interest. Whether you like it or not, this is just the smartest way to go about intelligence gathering. After all, if you know absolutely everything about everyone everywhere, you will rarely be caught out by anything.

The Implications of NSA Total Information Awareness for Cryptocurrency

At this point, you might be asking yourself how what has been a short crash course in NSA spying history pertains to the world of cryptocurrency today. In reality, though, the implications are simple.

Safe storage of any form of digital currency relies absolutely on devices where such currency is stored being impenetrable to hackers and other malicious third parties. As it stands, it can be proven without doubt that American three-letter agencies like the NSA have strived to have clandestine physical and software-based access to all consumer computing electronics and military-grade computing devices for at least the past two decades.

If your hardware wallet runs using a chip from ARM, your security is compromised. If your laptop runs an AMD or Intel CPU, your security is compromised.

It is worth considering also that when Satoshi Nakamoto created Bitcoin, he chose to use a type of encryption called SHA-256 to encrypt Bitcoin transaction blocks. However, he could have chosen to use far stronger SHA-512 encryption. Neither forms of encryption have yet been proven to have been broken. Use of SHA-512 encryption, though, would have at least made Bitcoin a little more future-proof.

Let's remember, though, that as we know from Microsoft and the NSA Key saga of 1999, the NSA expressly prohibits the export of technologies from the United States which utilize encryption technologies which the NSA itself can't already crack. Maybe it was the case that SHA-256 could be cracked at the time, but SHA-512 was still a little more difficult? After all, if you were Satoshi Nakamoto, why wouldn't you future-proof Bitcoin as best you could while you had the chance to?

In either case, there is no such thing as a cryptocurrency cipher the NSA cannot break or bypass via embedded technologies to confiscate any crypto you own if they want to. At present, if you own cryptocurrency, you are just being allowed to own it in the same way that countries like Libya and Iran spent 20+ years believing that using Crypto AG technologies allowed them to communicate secretly.

This is why, for now and in the future, a sound mind will always realize that cryptocurrency has no real inherent value. It's called cryptocurrency to sound secure. In reality, it's far less secure than any medium of exchange that humans have ever invented because someone made it that way before you even thought about buying it.

Cryptocurrency Is Not a Hedge Against the Coming Financial Crisis

Imagine building a city in China capable of housing millions of people, only for the entire city to immediately become a ghost city slowly surrendering back to nature. Now imagine building several such cities, only for the same to happen to each.

Imagine once being one of the biggest industrial powers on the planet like the United Kingdom once was. Now imagine dismantling all your industry as part of a thirty-year plan to transition to a purely financial services economy, only for places like Saudi Arabia and Dubai to take the crown of being the most tax-friendly and financial services-friendly places to do business.

Imagine being a country like America with the biggest economy on the planet, but also being in $38 trillion of debt, with 1 in 8 people being dependent on food stamps. Now imagine an entire world financial market increasingly underpinned by the health of tech stocks. As long as there is a new iPhone, NVIDIA graphics card, or Tesla tech launch on the horizon, the world economy is healthy. The minute there isn't, no one is really sure what will happen.

Make no mistake, the global economy is on borrowed time. Don't worry, though. According to increasing numbers of economic pundits, there may be a way for individuals, businesses, and whole countries to weather the storm ahead. The solution to coming financial chaos? Cryptocurrency, of course.

The Rise of Cryptocurrency Strategic Reserves

It's happening in El Salvador. It's happening in Texas. It's happening in Wyoming. It's happening in Luxembourg and the Czech Republic. It's even happening in Ethiopia and the Kingdom of Bhutan. To help combat inflation and to hedge against future global economic downturns, individual federal states, corporations, and some sovereign nations are beginning to create strategic cryptocurrency reserves. Their rationale for doing so is simple.

In the sixteen years since Bitcoin first hit exchanges, its value has skyrocketed. At the same time, the purchasing power of currencies like the U.S. dollar has diminished exponentially. Some people, therefore, see sovereign nations investing long-term in cryptocurrencies like Bitcoin as an easy way to offset inflation. Doing so, the same people argue, might even help pay off some countries' spiraling national debt obligations one day.

What if I told you, though, that we don't need a high-tech digital solution to spiraling debt and out-of-control inflation?

The Capitalism Con

In the West, we are told that we live in a capitalist society. This is one in which private individuals and businesses own the basic means of production, and the accumulation of wealth is dependent on individual ingenuity, supply, demand, competitiveness, and the ability of every individual to make economic decisions freely.

Stay true to the fundamental principles of capitalism (one of which is minimal government interference with the economy), and the economy flourishes. Sadly, neither the United States, UK, nor Europe can be called truly capitalist today.

To demonstrate, if you own a business and you get into debt which you are unable to service, or you make poor investment decisions which result in major losses, your business will fail. In the case of a store in a busy town or city center, a business failing in the past would usually see another quickly take its place. However, today we have a problem.

If we go back in time to the 2008 financial crisis, we go back to a period when suddenly, some businesses were called too big to fail. These were typically banks and included the likes of JP Morgan Chase, the United States' biggest bank, biggest mortgage lender, biggest commercial real estate owner, and biggest multifamily housing property owner.

As per the rules of true capitalism, if JP Morgan Chase was allowed to fail in 2008 just like any regular business, the financial world wouldn't have ended. Instead, a plethora of smaller banks, entrepreneurs, and still-solvent investors would simply have rushed to bid for assets on JP Morgan Chase's balance sheets.

Unlike today, where one giant bank known for financial recklessness dominates the American real estate and the low-income family rental market, we would instead have several smaller banks, all of which would be competing to acquire customers. This would see American banks offer better mortgage rates, commercial property rents would be priced more competitively, and most Americans would benefit from an overall lower cost of living.

In simple terms, more small banks increase competitiveness and economic equity, whereas having one giant bank hold sway over rental and mortgage markets just allows that bank to slowly strangle the economy. This isn't capitalism. In fact, bailouts in 2008 which saw the United States, UK, and Europe gift major banks taxpayer cash to cover losses were really the equivalent of Western powers giving CPR to several economic mass murderers. That said, not everyone followed the United States and Europe's lead when tackling the 2008 financial crisis.

The Iceland Equation

During the time between 2008 and 2010, it wasn't just Bitcoin which was invisible on the radar of the world news. During this time, so too was a small country called Iceland. This was because during the 2008 financial crisis, Iceland committed financial heresy.

While major banks in the UK and Europe and several central banks like those of Spain, Greece, and Cyprus were waiting in line for bailouts and European Central Bank rescue packages, Iceland decided to buck the trend. Iceland also did so in a way spectacularly true to the ideals of true capitalism and true democracy.

First, Iceland held a referendum. This saw the Icelandic government ask the population of Iceland whether they wanted a bailout from Europe or not. In response, the people of Iceland said no. Iceland subsequently allowed its banks to fail. This saw any debt which Icelandic banks owed overseas written off during formal bankruptcy proceedings.

New banks were established in the absence of Iceland's legacy banks, and all native Icelandic citizens' deposits were protected by the Icelandic government. Taxes didn't rise exponentially like they were at the same time in places like Greece. Suicides among the elderly, like were also happening in Greece, didn't happen, and no Icelandic homes and very few Icelandic businesses were foreclosed upon. This despite thousands of Americans being foreclosed upon at the same time.

After allowing its banks to collapse without taking on their debt burdens, Iceland became the fastest-growing economy in Europe, and this was why Iceland was effectively banned from the news during the aftermath of the 2008 financial crisis. After all, if Iceland could simply cancel its debts and return to growth so quickly, why couldn't your country?

Who Is Everyone in Debt to Anyway?

While Iceland was surreptitiously missing from the news for a few years between 2008 and 2011, thousands of people in America started living in cars, millions of people in the UK became accustomed to eating donated and out-of-date food from food banks, and all of Europe was told to work harder and retire later, because everyone was in debt to someone. Who exactly, though, is everyone indebted to?

As it stands, and as silly as it sounds, most of the West is in debt to itself. The United States, for example, has borrowed from the Federal Reserve. It has also borrowed against U.S. pensions, mutual funds, and domestic savings bonds, essentially gifting to itself the funds it needs today, while promising to pay back what it has taken from such pensions, mutual bonds, and savings bonds one day in the future. To make this exponentially clear, only 22% of America's current $38 trillion debt is owed to foreign governments and investors. The rest, America literally owes to itself.

Yes, it really is that simple. When your government says they need to increase taxes, create new taxes, or do whatever is necessary to fill big budgetary black holes in public finances, it's because they've already spent your pension, and the taxes you and your children are predicted to pay tomorrow, and now they need to tax you more to repay what they have taken.

As Henry Ford once famously said:

- **"It is perhaps well enough that the people of the nation do not know or understand our banking and monetary**

> **system, for if they did I believe there would be a revolution before tomorrow morning."**

Make no mistake, this is also why when Satoshi Nakamoto mined the original Bitcoin genesis block, he also included the message:

- "The Times 03/Jan/2009. Chancellor on brink of second bailout for banks."

NSA plant or new monetary system savant, Satoshi definitely knew what he was alluding to, even if some of his contemporaries at the time didn't.

Cryptocurrency Strategic Reserves Are Doomed to Fail

The words of Henry Ford are arguably truer today than they were a century ago. Almost no one today is aware of how our current monetary system works. One thing is for certain, though. When governments propose creating strategic cryptocurrency reserves to combat inflation and looming national debt crises, they are just proving that they have no idea how the current economy works either.

Let's remember that at any one moment, it is miners based in China who are processing almost 50% of all cryptocurrency transactions. A 51% attack on a cryptocurrency like Bitcoin originating from China is subsequently a very real possibility. Let's also remember that if Chinese miners were to ever stage such an attack, it wouldn't matter if a country like America kept its Bitcoin strategic reserve holdings in a hardware wallet in Fort Knox, or in an impenetrable nuclear bunker under Mount Shasta.

All a perpetrator of a 51% attack on any cryptocurrency has to do to steal your funds is reverse any transactions on the cryptocurrency transaction ledger in question which saw funds get deposited into your hardware wallet in the first place.

We have also already seen how Bitcoin miners in China can prevent Bitcoin transactions from settling, even without staging a 51% attack on the Bitcoin blockchain. What happens, in this case, if the United States and China ever go head to head in a hot war, rather than an economic war like the one which they are engaged in already?

Let's not bully China, though. The fact that 50% of cryptocurrency mining power is consolidated in any one nation-state makes the very idea of anyone creating cryptocurrency strategic reserves preposterous. Such reserves only work when cryptocurrency is truly decentralized, and the simple fact is that while proponents call coins like Bitcoin permissionless, peer-to-peer, and decentralized, none of this has been true for over a decade.

When proposing cryptocurrency strategic reserves, governments and major financial institutions are simply thinking with dollar signs, not real logic. The last Bitcoin that will ever be mined is predicted to be mined around the year 2140. Proponents of cryptocurrency strategic reserves, therefore, cite the fact that because Bitcoin is deflationary, Bitcoin can only increase in value until this time. However, let's be realistic here.

A hundred years ago, the horse and cart were still most people's primary mode of transport. If you worked in the city, a shoe shine boy would be sat outside your building who you could pay a few cents to free your shoes of the manure you'd accumulated just crossing the street. In less than a century, we've gone from shoe shine boys to space shuttles. Who knows, therefore, where technology might take us by 2140? In fact, it is folly to think that Bitcoin will still even be a thing.

Bitcoin today is barely 17 years old and is already facing major technological challenges posed by exponentially advancing artificial intelligence, quantum computing, and excruciatingly slow updatability. One can, therefore, only wonder what new challenges will present themselves in coming decades.

In a way, cryptocurrency has just become a new way to financially confuse people. The simple fact is, we don't need an asset that can magically increase forever in value to rid us of inflation and crippling national debt. We already have gold. When the next major financial crisis arrives, the most logical thing governments should do is cancel any unserviceable debts like Iceland did in 2008, and dispense with the pseudo-science bastardization of capitalism which sees any business or financial institution deemed too big to fail.

The Cryptocurrency as a Financial Safe Haven Myth

While governments and financial asset managers are scrambling to create strategic cryptocurrency reserves, individual investors are also being encouraged to turn to digital assets to hedge against coming financial Armageddon. Pundits who propose using digital assets to safeguard personal wealth during an economic collapse often refer to coins like Bitcoin as the equivalent of digital gold. In doing so, they suggest that during financial market downturns, Bitcoin retains its value like gold usually does, while stocks and real estate start to depreciate.

In reality, while Bitcoin has risen exponentially in value since 2009, Bitcoin also follows the regular financial markets and often behaves similarly to major tech stocks.

When tech stocks start falling in value, history shows us that Bitcoin usually does too. Worse, when new-to-market investors see Bitcoin prices start to reverse on exchanges, the majority panic sell. This results in catastrophic price corrections which often don't start to reverse until the next Bitcoin halving event. In no way, therefore, can Bitcoin be likened to conventional assets like precious metals.

Let's put this in perspective. Let's assume that a magical money fairy visits you tonight to tell you that a global financial collapse that will make that of 2008 look pale in comparison will start tomorrow. You now have two choices. You can choose to hedge against this crisis by investing in Bitcoin, or you can invest in gold or real estate.

Whatever asset you invest in will depreciate in value when tomorrow's crisis hits. People will start selling gold to pay bills. Bursting of real estate bubbles will see whatever property you buy depreciate in value. Bitcoin investors will also start selling to pay bills, and when this happens, new-to-market investors will panic sell, resulting in any Bitcoin you buy today depreciating by as much as 50% or even 75% over coming weeks and months.

With the next Bitcoin halving event scheduled for 2028, you can be reasonably sure that you will eventually recoup any losses and perhaps even double whatever money you put into Bitcoin today by 2029. However, you can't touch your Bitcoin during this time. There are also other variables to consider.

What if Bitcoin still doesn't harden itself against quantum computing by 2028 and quantum computing manifests as a threat by then? What also happens if America and China engage in a hot war or a more hostile cold war which sees Chinese Bitcoin miners attempt a 51% attack against the Bitcoin blockchain?

What happens between now and 2028 if you just lose your Bitcoin private key?

If you invest in gold, you will at least own something tangible which has been steadily appreciating in value since the beginning of recorded history.

If you invest in real estate, you might find that the value of your property diminishes by 25% or 50% or 70% during a Great Depression-like economic downturn. However, you will still have an asset which you can recoup losses from by putting it on the rental market, and it will likely recover in value eventually, provided you maintain it.

All this being the case, what do you choose to invest in when the magical money fairy gives you the heads-up? If you think about it logically, Bitcoin and cryptocurrency present the biggest risk.

Remember, it really is just software.

What If Cryptocurrency Causes the Next Great Crisis?

Hopefully, it is clear how the creation of cryptocurrency strategic reserves by nation-states and how using cryptocurrency as a safe haven to hedge against coming future financial collapses deserves a little more forethought than proponents currently argue. However, there is something else which deserves discussion. Namely, what if it is cryptocurrency itself which triggers the next great financial crisis in the first place?

What if this was even the intended purpose of legacy cryptocurrencies all along?

How Cryptocurrency Is Fast Evolving Into 1984 Nightmare Cash

Bitcoin's eventual arrival on the world stage in late 2010 wasn't exactly met with mass fanfare. It likely would have been 2 years earlier when the Occupy movement was seeing tent cities establish themselves in the middle of Wall Street and the City of London. However, by the time that Bitcoin was dragged into the media spotlight by Wikileaks, the Occupy movement was long since over. Any spirit of mass rebellion against the prevailing financial system had also long since evaporated.

People were tired. Every day they were reminded that they were poor, while simultaneously being bombarded with confusing financial spin and complete gibberish to explain why the world was in financial ruin. Words like "Bitcoin" and terms like "decentralization" and "blockchain" sounded similar to such gibberish.

How Bitcoin Went From Zero to Hero

Thankfully, in the years following 2010, especially those between 2011 and 2017, people did start to take interest in Bitcoin. The reason why was simple. By 2015, this curious thing that banks and governments derided as "air money" was trading at over $1,000 per coin. Cursory research into the economic mechanics of Bitcoin was also enough to convince many people that future returns on investments were guaranteed.

Bitcoin has a finite supply. Most of the Bitcoin that will ever be minted is already in circulation, and the amount of new Bitcoin entering circulation diminishes by 50% every four years. As Bitcoin scarcity increases, so, therefore, does the value of Bitcoin. The years between 2009 and 2015 proved that Bitcoin was working exactly as per this design. Investing $1,000 in Bitcoin in 2015 could, therefore, conceivably see people make easy 100% or even 1,000% returns in just a few years. And many people did.

I have stated repeatedly that cryptocurrencies like Bitcoin only have value if people believe them to have value, and in the run-up to 2020, belief in Bitcoin became contagious. In fact, we are now at a point where Bitcoin is considered a mainstay in modern finance.

How Bitcoin and cryptocurrency work is still a mystery to most people. However, Bitcoin has effectively gone mainstream. When financial advisors suggest incorporating a little Bitcoin into retirement funds, most people subsequently say yes without thinking. Bitcoin is that thing, after all, that made a lot of people very rich, that many people wish they hadn't been so cautious about in the beginning.

Presently, belief in Bitcoin is so strong that major companies, institutions, and even governments are incorporating Bitcoin into financial portfolios and strategic reserves. Stablecoin cryptocurrencies like Tether (USDT) are even praised by the likes of Donald Trump's Genius Act as helping strengthen the U.S. dollar and overall U.S. national security. There is just one problem.

As a basic Wall Street rule, when hype around any asset class reaches the point which cryptocurrency has, it is usually a sign that a major market correction is coming.

Is Donald Trump This Generation's Shoeshine Boy?

Is the crypto party about to end? As a famous story in Wall Street circles goes, at the height of America's 1920s economic boom, the stockbroker Joseph Kennedy Sr. (the father of JFK) was walking up Wall Street. On his way, Kennedy Sr. decided to have his shoes polished by a local shoeshine boy. To his amusement, while the shoeshine boy Kennedy chose was working, the boy began listing his own stock picks for the day.

While amused at first, Kennedy Sr. quickly realized that if even the shoeshine boys on the street knew what stocks were booming, it was probably time to get out of the market. This Kennedy Sr. did, just days before the stock market was wiped out in what became the start of the Great Depression.

When I refer to Donald Trump as this generation's shoeshine boy, I do so because it seems like Trump is jumping himself and America into the crypto party, just because he's heard good things about it, not because he knows very much about it, or what time the party is scheduled to end.

After officially taking office in January 2025, President Donald Trump immediately began pressuring the U.S. House of Representatives to pass what has since become known as the Genius Act. Now passed into law, this legislation, according to Trump himself:

"is going to make America the **UNDISPUTED** Leader in Digital Assets — Nobody will do it better, it is pure **GENIUS!** Digital Assets are the future, and our Nation is going to own it. We are talking about **MASSIVE** Investment, and Big Innovation."

"Get it to my desk, **ASAP**," Trump demanded in June 2025. **"NO DELAYS, NO ADD-ONS**. This is American Brilliance at its best, and we are going to show the World how to WIN with Digital Assets like never before!"

When the Act eventually passed, Donald Trump quickly thanked Tether CEO Paolo Ardoino for his support. He was also able to do so in person, thanks to having invited Ardoino and other crypto industry representatives to the East Room of the White House to celebrate the Genius Act passing.

What is the Genius Act?

At its most basic, the Genius Act forces any stablecoin issuer in the United States to prove via regular audits that they hold enough U.S. dollars or an equivalent amount of short-term U.S. Treasury bonds to back all stablecoins they issue. The Act also requires stablecoin issuers to possess the ability to freeze and burn any stablecoins suspected as being used for illicit purposes. It also requires stablecoin issuers to verify the identities of anyone buying stablecoins.

Providing that stablecoin issuers can comply with the Genius Act, the Act itself effectively makes it possible for any U.S. business and even foreign businesses (providing they hold real USD reserves or equivalent U.S. Treasuries) to now issue digital U.S. dollars.

Independently of the Genius Act, President Donald Trump has also signed an executive order mandating that the United States create its own strategic reserve of Bitcoin and other digital assets.

Did Trump Just Destabilize the Dollar?

As a businessman, Donald Trump must surely be able to weigh risk when investing in or promoting any asset. This being the case, he must surely be aware that Tether Limited, an offshore company behind the world's biggest stablecoin Tether, constantly resists being independently audited. He must also be aware that Tether once partnered with the disgraced crypto money launderer Sam Bankman-Fried and that Tether itself is masterminded by a cabal of shadowy figures with various discredited credentials and backstories.

Why in this case, was Tether's CEO invited to the White House to celebrate the Genius Act passing?

Putting Tether aside, anyone who knows just a little U.S. history will also see that the Genius Act parallels how America's banking system worked from 1830 until the advent of the American Civil War. During this time, any wealthy individual could open a bank and issue U.S. dollars, providing that any dollar issued was backed by an equivalent amount of real gold or other assets. There was just one problem.

Such a decentralized banking system depends on the infallibility of regular independent audits. America's Free Banking system subsequently failed due to too many banks failing to pass audits, too many operating irregularly, numerous subsequent bank runs, and the eventual destabilization of the dollar itself.

To put this in perspective, using a U.S. dollar issued in Michigan in 1850 was not the same as using a U.S. dollar issued in New York. In Michigan, banks were regularly collapsing due to bank runs following rumors that they weren't holding sufficient gold to back money they were issuing. In New York, though, regulatory oversight was much more stringent, resulting in better depositor confidence.

Try to use a New York bank-issued dollar in Washington and there would rarely be a problem. However, if you were to try and pay for goods with a Michigan-issued dollar, a store proprietor might refuse to accept payment, or they might impose a surcharge to cover potential losses when banking your Michigan dollar later.

The Genius Act effectively reprises this almost two-century-defunct form of currency issuance. To put this in perspective, the likes of Tesla, Amazon, or Facebook, or your wealthy neighbor next door, can now easily create and issue their own digital dollar. What happens though if Facebook's stock starts to decline in value and overnight Facebook becomes this generation's MySpace due to some new social media market innovator?

The Genius Act says that this won't affect the price of a theoretical Facebook stablecoin. Facebook, after all, would still have to prove that it has enough collateral to back every coin ever issued. However, one can be sure that if stock prices of major companies issuing stablecoins go down, this will spook stablecoin holders into switching quickly to other stablecoins and other digital assets. In effect, digital dollar bank runs will likely become commonplace.

To pardon the pun, you don't need to be a genius to understand the inherent problems with the Genius Act. Nor do you have to be a genius to understand why the United States creating a Bitcoin strategic reserve makes no sense. China dominates 50% of Bitcoin mining. This means that China owns your Bitcoin unless you are willing to invest in mining on an equivalent scale yourself.

Make no mistake. If the average American was more cognizant of how cryptocurrency works, Trump would have been impeached for even proposing legislation like the Genius Act.

Stablecoins Are Not America's Get out of Debt Free Card

Because the sale of short-term U.S. treasuries is fundamental to the way the United States services its national debt, it is easy to understand what Trump might hope to achieve with the Genius Act.

Trump essentially wants to transform as much of America's debt as he can into cryptocurrency stablecoins. In theory, this will strengthen the position of the U.S. dollar as the world's reserve currency. In reality, though, using stablecoins in this way actually exposes the U.S. bond market to a significant level of risk.

As already discussed, Tether, the world's most popular stablecoin at present, holds more U.S. short-term securities than Germany and South Korea. However, increasing numbers of people doubt that Tether really holds enough cash, or cash equivalents, in reserve to cover even a fraction of the amount of Tether in circulation. This is a problem as if Tether or any other stablecoin issuer ever collapses while holding a significant amount of U.S. Treasuries (as the Genius Act requires), this could destabilize the U.S. bond market itself.

According to a 2025 Bank for International Settlements (BIS) paper, "Stablecoins and Safe Asset Prices," by Rashad Ahmed and Iñaki Aldasoro, a run on or collapse of Tether could destabilize the entire U.S. bond market.

In their paper, Ahmed and Aldasoro give a conservative estimate that a Tether collapse might result in a fire sale of short-dated U.S. securities. This is where holders of short-term bonds expect them to fall in value and attempt to sell everything they hold as quickly as possible. However, both researchers make clear that nothing like a Tether collapse has ever occurred previously. A worst-case scenario could, therefore, see a parabolic run on U.S. securities. This would be where a fire sale might escalate into a complete loss of confidence in the U.S. bond market, resulting in longer-term bonds being dumped by investors.

As U.S. Treasuries are used to service the United States' national debt, a parabolic run on securities would have a significant adverse impact on the real-world economy.

There is, of course, the argument to be made that because Tether refuses to be audited, the Genius Act effectively prohibits Tether from now being listed on United States cryptocurrency exchanges like Coinbase. However, a peculiar and very obvious loophole in the Genius Act expressly allows Tether and other unregulated stablecoins to continue to operate on decentralized exchanges. Namely, exchanges like those which make up the entirety of the Decentralized Finance (DeFi) market. (Think exchanges like Uniswap, SushiSwap, and PancakeSwap hosted on the Ethereum blockchain.)

Are Genius Act Stablecoins Just CBDCs by the Back Door?

Now that the Genius Act has passed, companies like X, formerly Twitter, and Meta, the parent company of Facebook, are already racing to create their own Genius Act-compliant stablecoins. This, being the case, it is looking increasingly likely that Trump's Genius Act of 2025 might have just laid the red carpet out for Central Bank Digital Currencies via the back door.

For several decades, the United States has upheld a prohibition on non-financial businesses like Facebook from acquiring and thereby acting as financial services businesses. Facebook attempted to create its own stablecoin, Libra, just a few years ago. However, Facebook was ultimately prevented from doing so by laws similar to those which separate church and state, but laws which instead separate tech companies and fintech companies.

There were good reasons for these laws. As we have previously discussed, there are limits today on how much your bank can know about you. Legally, your bank must be able to verify your identity. However, your bank doesn't have real-time knowledge of your location, what you are wearing, what you are talking about, who you vote for, or who your friends are.

Thanks to the Genius Act, your bank—or at least a service like Facebook that you might soon use like a bank—will know everything about you. It is also likely that many people will start to transition to using social media companies as banking providers when such companies start issuing stablecoins. This is thanks to the fact that while stablecoins are not allowed to accrue interest, issuers are allowed to offer interest-like rewards in return for their usage.

To demonstrate, regular U.S. dollars deposited in regular U.S. bank accounts typically generate a 0.40% to 1.71% rate of interest. By comparison, the cryptocurrency exchange Coinbase already offers users of the stablecoin Circle yield-like rewards of 4.1% on any Circle balance held in a Coinbase wallet. It is, therefore, easy to see how cryptocurrency exchanges and tech companies like Google and X will be able to incentivize people into using stablecoins over regular cash.

At present, the only real obstacle which stands in the way of big-tech-issued stablecoins becoming the equivalent of Central Bank Digital Currencies (or a significant prelude to these) is the U.S. Consumer Financial Protection Bureau (CFPB). It is, therefore, worth noting that in tandem with the creation of the Genius Act, the current Trump administration has attempted to fire the entire staff of the Consumer Financial Protection Bureau. After failing to find a legal way to do so, the same Trump administration is now litigating against the National Treasury Employees Union in an effort to disband the CFPB via other means.

In case it isn't obvious, the Consumer Financial Protection Bureau is the very bureau which could prevent companies like Facebook from using metadata sourced from social media profiles to determine things like what yield-like rewards you qualify for, what other financial services you might be eligible for, and even how, when, and where you spend your stablecoins in the first place.

Most Americans would likely agree that such protections would be a good thing. They just wouldn't be good for stablecoin issuers like Facebook or X. This also might be why Elon Musk, during his time as head of the Department of Government Efficiency (DOGE), made the CFPB one of his very first defunding targets.

What Is the Planned Endgame for Legacy Cryptocurrency?

As of September 2024, 134 countries representing 98% of the global economy were actively investigating ways to transition to a purely digital currency standard. However, very few people are aware of their governments' plans to completely flip our current currency paradigm. Tell the average person on the street that there might be no such thing as cash a few years from now, and they simply won't believe you.

Ignorance concerning just how soon Central Bank Digital Currencies might be implemented is by no means accidental. Governments know digital currencies won't be popular. Implementation of Central Bank Digital Currencies must, therefore, not appear planned. Rather, their rollout must look necessary. Ideally, some kind of crisis must present itself which makes their implementation absolutely incontrovertible. However, banks and governments also have another problem. Put simply, the world already has over 20,000 different forms of digital currency. Why, therefore, do we need any more?

The Highly Likely Coming Crypto Crisis

In The Crypto Con, I have reiterated several times how it is my belief that Bitcoin itself was likely created by a three-letter agency like the NSA. It is also my belief that the chief goal of cryptocurrency as we know it has been to slowly condition global populaces to accept an eventual cashless future brought about by the implementation of Central Bank Digital Currencies.

The problem with Central Bank Digital Currencies is that CBDCs themselves cannot logically exist in tandem with legacy cryptocurrencies like Bitcoin. After all, if people have a choice between using CBDCs, which they will know will track their every purchase and which can be programmed to prohibit certain purchases, people will logically shift to using legacy cryptocurrencies like Bitcoin.

To prevent any such shift from happening, something must logically happen first which inspires total loss of confidence in legacy cryptocurrencies. There has to, if you like, be some kind of cataclysm which wipes out the current cryptocurrency market completely.

What Might Cause a Complete Crypto Collapse?

Almost all legacy cryptocurrencies currently on the market are susceptible to a range of technological vulnerabilities which I have already discussed at length.

As cryptocurrency mining continues to be consolidated in China, very little stands in the way of China one day staging a 51% attack against market-leading cryptocurrencies like Bitcoin. This would see investor confidence in Bitcoin evaporate. However, this wouldn't necessarily see confidence in the entire cryptocurrency market falter.

To rid the world of the menace of decentralized digital currencies more completely, an agency like the NSA could make use of hardware backdoors in all modern personal and business computers (like the Intel Management Engine) to disrupt several forms of cryptocurrency simultaneously. Making use of what would effectively be the biggest botnet the world has ever seen, the NSA—or even just Intel—could stage massive denial-of-service attacks on all known cryptocurrency transaction nodes and mining farms.

Naturally, the likes of China or Russia would be blamed for such an attack. The only problem is that there will be PR hell to pay later if some plucky NSA insider like Edward Snowden ever decides to snitch about the existence of such botnets and backdoors and how they have been used against the masses.

Thankfully, there are less extreme technological options available when it comes to taking down the legacy cryptocurrency market.

Tether as a Possible Crypto Market Time Bomb

When discussing Donald Trump's Genius Act in the previous chapter, I made it clear how this Act requires all stablecoin providers operating in the United States to hold real U.S. dollar reserves or an equivalent amount of short-term U.S. Treasuries representative of every stablecoin they make available.

What is curious about the Genius Act is that Tether, the world's biggest stablecoin by market capitalization, was already using U.S. Treasuries to partially back Tether stablecoins long before the Genius Act was announced. Currently owning more U.S. Treasury bonds than whole countries like Germany and South Korea, Switzerland's Bank of International Settlements has already questioned what a theoretical Tether collapse might mean for the U.S. Treasuries market itself.

Cryptocurrency industry insiders like Justin Bons, founder of Europe's oldest cryptocurrency fund, Cyber Capital, are also certain that a Tether collapse is on the horizon.

Bons claims that when Tether collapses, it will make the collapse of Sam Bankman-Fried's FTX and the collapse of Bernie Madoff's infamous 2008 Wall Street Ponzi scheme look like small change being lost down the side of the sofa. Tether going down will, after all, wipe at least

$118 billion from the cryptocurrency market instantly. There is also no way of knowing until a collapse happens just how much prices of coins like Bitcoin and Ethereum have been artificially inflated since 2015 by Tether's monthly money printing.

As independent cryptocurrency analysts at Chain Mind have also stated, "Tether isn't collapsing today, but the risk is real. It will happen suddenly—when it happens."

To put this in perspective, it was losses of approximately $1.4 trillion linked to defaults on U.S. mortgages which triggered the 2008 financial collapse. By comparison, Bitcoin alone now has a market capitalization of over $1.7 trillion, with the cryptocurrency market overall being valued at $3.7 trillion.

If it is ever revealed that Tether really has been printing Tether stablecoins which it cannot back with real dollar reserves, simply to create artificial market demand for Bitcoin, complete cryptocurrency market carnage will ensue. This carnage will also be contagious.

To make this as simple as possible to understand, the $1.4 trillion linked to mortgage defaults which triggered the 2008 financial crisis was $1.4 trillion of loans made available by banks like JP Morgan Chase, which were expected to be repaid with interest, but which weren't.

Bitcoin having a market capitalization of $1.7 trillion means that $1.7 trillion has been used to buy Bitcoin by millions of people and businesses, all of whom expect to make a return on their investment by the price of Bitcoin continuing to rise higher.

To make matters worse, as of September 2025, over 200 U.S. companies have adopted digital asset treasury/strategic reserve strategies, 190 of these either predominantly or exclusively hold Bitcoin. 200 companies might not sound like a significant number. However, each has an exposure to the cryptocurrency market ranging from tens to hundreds of millions of dollars. Several U.S. states, overseas businesses, and even nation-states have created similar reserves. What, therefore, happens if Bitcoin suddenly drops from near $100,000 in value to a mere $10,000 or $20,000, with it having no hope of prices recovering for another decade once Tether is out of the market?

If true demand was always largely artificial, this might happen. Worse, Bitcoin mining farms might suddenly find mining Bitcoin unprofitable. This could result in mining Bitcoin becoming more decentralized, but it could also see Bitcoin mining nearly abandoned, resulting in prices falling even further.

How the Bitcoin Mythos Will Probably Go Full Circle

The Bitcoin mythos which the general public is presented with is as simple as it is romantic. Bitcoin, digital currency proponents claim, was born out of grassroots rebellion against mass bank fraud and gross government mismanagement of the economy which cumulatively resulted in the 2008 financial crisis. (Let's just forget about the fact that no one really knew about Bitcoin until late 2010.)

The hero of this crisis? Satoshi Nakamoto, a lone genius who rose like an anonymous digital phoenix out of the ashes of the 2008 financial markets with a brand-new kind of ungovernable, uncounterfeitable, inherently deflationary, and inherently democratic new kind of currency.

Fast forward to 2025, and we now have the very real possibility that the world is sitting on a new economic bomb, the fuse of which might be cryptocurrency itself.

Every day that Tether resists being independently audited (despite promises to submit to an audit going back as far as 2015), suspicions rise that Tether really has been printing digital money out of thin air and artificially inflating the price of Bitcoin and other cryptocurrencies for the past decade.

Should these suspicions ever be verified, it is no longer just a few hundred computer nerds on an obscure Internet forum who will lose money. Rather, the economic shock wave will reverberate through the regular stock market, the U.S. Treasuries market, and beyond.

Cryptocurrency exchanges valued more than Walmart will collapse. Thanks to regulatory changes pushed by the U.S. Federal Housing Finance Agency (FHFA) which allow new home buyers to use cryptocurrency as collateral on loans, even major mortgage lenders like Fannie Mae and Freddie Mac have exposure to the current crypto market.

Literally everything from AI stocks to the U.S. housing market will be impacted, and 2008 will start to repeat. The only question is, what new kind of currency will be presented as the world's savior this time?

What the End of Legacy Cryptocurrency Might Look Like

Central Bank Digital Currencies have always been coming. As soon as we had barcodes on food, they were on the digital horizon.

Donald Trump's Genius Act, which I discussed in the last chapter, is just one way they may become an economic reality for everyone, especially if people have the chance to earn 4% rewards on new stablecoin dollar balances, as opposed to a measly 0.7% rate of interest which they might get on non-digital dollar balances held by banks.

All the world needs first, if programmable stablecoins and CBDCs are to become the world's next currency standard, replacing cash completely, is a big enough crisis to give people one final nudge toward their acceptance.

Should Tether collapse, this final nudge won't really be a nudge. Likely, there will be an incomparable sense of panic which sweeps through the crypto market and regular financial markets simultaneously.

Overnight, the 18th biggest buyer of U.S. securities will vanish. Confidence in U.S. securities will evaporate, as market pundits point out that Tether was obviously a scam which the U.S. was more than foolhardy ever getting into bed with. A devaluing of the U.S. dollar will follow, with this happening in tandem with massive devaluing of all cryptocurrencies and all stocks in companies with exposure to the cryptocurrency market.

In the blink of an eye, every investor and financial guru who was ever hostile toward the idea of cryptocurrency will be vindicated. As it becomes known that the true price of Bitcoin has been greatly exaggerated thanks to unchecked Tether printing, each will laud what is fast becoming a complete global financial collapse as always being inevitable. Crypto millionaires will have their net worth obliterated, and to insulate their own currencies from total loss of confidence in cryptocurrency and possibly the U.S. dollar, several countries will rush to pass laws prohibiting unregulated cryptocurrency completely.

As all of this is happening, any cryptocurrency traders and investors not completely underwater will rush to liquidate what is left of their assets. Real-world runs on real-world banks will start, and it will then only be a matter of time before banks start limiting withdrawals to prevent their own collapse.

As soon as the solvency of real-world brick-and-mortar banks is threatened by the collapse of everything everywhere linked or even suspected to be linked to legacy cryptocurrencies, banks and governments will make their move.

As the dust settles, there will be news of suicides, murders, and attacks on the likes of crypto influencers and crypto company CEOs. The world will also be told that what is happening isn't like any kind of boom-and-bust cycle the economy has seen previously. Rather, the public will be told simply that trillions of dollars' worth of global liquidity that has been pumped into Bitcoin and other digital assets over the past decade has blinked out of existence, literally in the blink of an eye.

This time, people will be told, the global economy really is irreparably broken—so broken that the only solution is a mass financial reset.

Enter Central Bank Digital Currencies

When the crypto market does fail, world governments will appear powerless to act. However, as the world descends into chaos, world leaders will eventually take to stages to announce a bold and innovative solution to the current crisis. Likely, this will be one that sees banks recapitalize by using what consumer deposits are left, before entire world currencies are reissued to depositors in the form of Central Bank Digital Currencies.

Special television broadcasts, online resources, and community presentations will teach people how to use the new digital currency being made available. At the same time, banks and governments will go to lengths to reassure the public that balances in their new digital wallets are much more secure than past iterations of digital currency like Bitcoin.

Bitcoin and cryptocurrencies like it, the powers that be will trumpet, failed because it was decentralized and not governed by any central authority. This was why, if you ever lost access to your Bitcoin balance, it was gone for good. This was why, scams like Tether were even ever possible in the first plasced. CBDC balances, on the other hand, will be recoverable if people ever lose access to their bank- or government-issued digital wallets.

The narrative which is used to create the new age of Central Bank Digital Currencies will be a simple one: yesterday's cryptocurrency was bad, and we told you so from the beginning because it wasn't centrally managed and overseen like ours is, but the technology was sound. We are just going to utilize it the right way.

Likely, populaces will initially welcome the world's new forms of digital currency. This will be especially true if several days go by during which time it is impossible to use an ATM or even transact with credit and debit cards. It will only be later, as traditions of putting cash in Christmas and birthday cards are remembered, and simple things like paying for groceries during power outages become things of the past, when people start to realize the nature of the new digital prison they live in. This, and that the whole point of bygone cryptocurrencies like Bitcoin, was to condition them to eventually accept their new prison of air in the first place.

Alternative Solutions to the Next Financial Crisis

Will a future collapse of the stablecoin Tether result in a financial domino effect that leads to the complete collapse of the current crypto market? Alternatively, might a rogue nation-state, three-letter government agency, or cabal of hackers one day decide to take down cryptocurrency for good by hijacking millions of consumer PCs via built-in Intel and AMD backdoors?

Whatever crypto catastrophe crosses the finish line first, one will manifest eventually. Mother Nature might even intervene in the interim, using something like a solar flare to bring chaos to the basic technology that underpins the current global economy.

Whatever crypto poison you pick, the simple fact is that a form of currency you can physically hold in your hand will always have more basic intrinsic value than any digital equivalent, centralized or decentralized. It is therefore important to understand that low-tech alternative solutions to cryptocurrencies have been used in the past to offset imminent financial crises. Two of the simplest and most effective of these have been the Greenback and the Bradbury Pound.

What Was the Bradbury Pound?

In 1914, when Great Britain declared war on Germany, the financial order of the UK was strikingly similar to that of the U.S. today.

Like the Federal Reserve today, the Bank of England was the only authority in the country that could issue currency. If the UK government needed cash, it had to borrow it from the Bank of England

and agree to repay any amount borrowed with interest. There was just one problem.

The outbreak of war sent the UK's private and public sectors into a panic. This led to a run on banks as people attempted to withdraw savings and liquidate assets and investments. Soon, gold-backed banknotes issued by the Bank of England were in short supply. Worse, continued withdrawals would have seen the Bank of England's stock of bullion backing notes start to diminish. This couldn't be allowed to happen. After all, the war against Germany and its allies would already be lost if Britain entered it bankrupt.

To stop this from happening, the UK government quickly passed the Currency and Bank Notes Act. This Act made it possible for the UK government to issue legal tender independently of the Bank of England, with all notes issued by the UK government backed by the "wealth and labor potential of the country."

Going into print immediately, the new Bradbury Pound had the same value as pounds issued by the Bank of England. However, unlike Bank of England banknotes, the Bradbury Pound was issued free of debt or interest. It was also accepted anywhere regular Bank of England notes were and played a crucial role in stabilizing the UK economy between 1914 and 1917.

What Happened in 1917?

Despite the Bradbury Pound being created to save the Bank of England from potential collapse, the privately owned Bank of England quickly realized that the Bradbury Pound was doing more harm than good—at least to itself. After all, the Bank of England was no longer collecting interest on new money entering circulation. In 1917, the UK government therefore ceased issuing new Bradbury Pounds and reverted to borrowing cash from the Bank of England whenever new cash injections into the economy or additional government borrowing was necessary. However, one thing must be made abundantly clear.

The years during which the Bradbury Pound circulated alongside Bank of England notes saw the country undertake massive infrastructure projects vital for preparing for and waging war. The Bradbury Pound was not, therefore, some kind of baseless IOU. It was a real currency with real value that created real value. However, the Bradbury Pound wasn't really an innovation in of itself.

The start of the American Civil War half a century earlier in 1861, hadn't just been the start of a war between the Northern and Southern states of the U.S. Rather, the start of the Civil War was also the start of a battle waged between different European banks for dominance over the future American economy.

At the start of the Civil War, England and France were hoping for a Southern, Confederate victory. However, neither country was willing to voice support for either side of the American conflict openly. They therefore waged war via economic means. This saw European banks offer to support Union forces in Washington financially, but only if the North American Union agreed to pay between 24% and 36% interest on any money borrowed.

Knowing that such a rate of interest would shackle America in debt for generations, President Abraham Lincoln refused these offers of assistance. Instead, he established a parallel currency to the existing gold-backed U.S. dollar. This currency took the form of green-colored paper dollar notes called Greenback dollars, which had the same value as regular U.S. dollars—they just weren't backed by or redeemable for gold. Instead, Greenbacks were backed by the word and honor of the United States federal government.

Banks in Europe were outraged by the creation of the Greenback. The Greenback, after all, set a precedent for governments creating money independently of banks, and this simply couldn't be allowed. In retaliation, 1862 saw Europe's banks start strategically selling U.S. securities in order to cause chaos on U.S. markets. However, the Greenback didn't just survive—it flourished.

As well as being used to fund 15% of the Union's conflict with the Confederate South, Greenbacks were used to pay everyday wages and buy everyday goods and services. In fact, due to the chaotic nature of the free banking era that still existed at the time, many Americans preferred using government-issued Greenbacks over bank-issued dollars, as the value of a Greenback was always guaranteed.

Greenback dollars were also officially recognized as legitimate currency by Tsar Alexander II of Russia, who supported the abolishment of slavery (a primary goal of the Civil War) and who even went so far as to dock Russian fleets in New York and San Francisco. This being done to warn Britain and France against providing military or monetary support to the Confederate South.

Thanks to the success of Greenbacks in helping stabilize the U.S. economy throughout the Civil War, Abraham Lincoln's administration quickly passed Acts like the National Banking Acts of 1863 and 1864. These put an end to the so-called free-banking era in America and created a uniform currency system administered directly by the now-unified federal government.

Sadly, on April 14, 1865—just five days after the official end of the Civil War—Lincoln was assassinated, and his successors quickly began dismantling these Acts while simultaneously consigning the Greenback itself to history.

Would Currencies Like the Bradbury Pound or Greenback Still Work Today?

In America, Donald Trump intends to use his GENIUS Act to essentially transform U.S. government debt into cryptocurrency stablecoins. However, as previously discussed, the GENIUS Act simply parallels how U.S. monetary policy worked in the pre-Civil War chaotic free-banking era. Adopting a monetary policy similar to that of Lincoln's Greenback or the UK's 1914 Currency and Bank Notes Act would make more sense. This way, only one currency paralleling the value of the dollar would enter circulation, as opposed to several that will all require constant independent auditing to remain viable.

As has also been previously discussed, we have the precedent of Iceland in 2008, which dealt with the then-global financial crisis by allowing its banks to fail and by writing off otherwise unpayable debts through formal bankruptcy proceedings.

With the national debt of the U.S. alone currently topping $38 trillion, it is folly to think that this will ever be repaid. If such an amount is to be repaid, the public also has a right to know exactly whom is being repaid what and why. Ideally, the public should also be asked via a referendum—like in Iceland—whether they agree to basic repayment terms.

In real life, being in debt isn't complicated. If you owe a bank or your government any amount of money, a court can only enforce collection if your bank or the government agency you owe can present proof of your debt and provide a full list of all associated charges and penalties. Governments should, therefore, not be allowed to refer to public debt burdens as obscure budgetary black holes or impossible-to-comprehend fiscal deficits. Any debt needs to be itemized and easy to understand.

Put simply, if it can't be itemized, independently scrutinized, or corroborated, debt can legally be written off as fraudulent—just like it was in Iceland.

Currency Should Always Be Comprehensible

When Bitcoin first began to go mainstream in late 2010, the vast majority of its critics were hostile to the very idea that anyone but global governments could create any kind of currency. All that most such critics didn't realize is that governments don't actually issue currency.

Even today, the average man or woman on the street still believes that the cash in their pocket is backed by real commodities like gold and silver. Very few people are aware that central banks actually issue cash, not governments—and even fewer people are aware that the cash we have today was decoupled from real commodities like gold over half a century ago.

The problem here is that if few people are capable of comprehending how our current monetary system works, even fewer will ever be capable of understanding how cryptocurrency works. Even fewer still will ever be capable of understanding how Central Bank Digital Currencies work.

This ignorance is bliss for central banks, whose ultimate agenda is to unify the digital identities of everyone everywhere with programmable cryptocurrencies, which, in turn, will see everyday life descend into a 1984-like state surveillance nightmare. To vanquish this nightmare before it starts, we therefore need to develop a currency standard that is low-tech, easy to understand, and easy for anyone anywhere to utilize. As it stands, the Bradbury Pound and Greenback represent two such proven-to-work currency standards.

One problem, of course, is that many countries like the UK have massively deindustrialized since the last century. The Bradbury Pound had value in 1914 that was pegged to the wealth and productivity of the British Isles as a nation. At that point, the UK landed more fresh fish annually than Japan, was one of the world's most accomplished shipbuilders, and was largely self-sufficient in terms of agriculture and energy production.

With all of this industry gone, a new Bradbury Pound today could still have its value pegged to the wealth and productivity of the nation (with the same being true for any country). However, countries would have to commit to new industry and infrastructure projects to breathe life into the currency.

Trickle-Down vs. Trickle-Up Economics

As well as being ignorant of how money itself works, the majority of Western populations today are also ignorant of how the economy itself works.

In any true capitalist economy, the economy performs best when government interference in economic policy is kept to a minimum. However, since the 1980s, Western governments have aggressively favored a supply-side-centric interpretation of basic economic theory known as trickle-down economics. Tax the wealthiest in society less, and proponents of trickle-down economics argue that wealth will eventually trickle down to the middle, working, and poorest classes of society.

In reality, very little trickles down through the economic classes. The wealthiest in society instead gradually buy up all real estate to monopolize the low-income housing market. Likewise, businesses and corporations try to protect their wealth by investing in things like automation, AI, and robotics to reduce everything from wage costs to future pension liabilities. The most wealthy in society also like to keep their wealth offshore, and when governments do attempt to raise taxes, they usually flee overseas completely.

Think about it logically. Money doesn't trickle down. Rather, someone is always paying it up. When you buy a burger at McDonald's, you are making McDonald's a little bit richer. It never ever works the other way around. Even if McDonald's gives you a coupon, you are still poorer after you buy your next Happy Meal.

As trickle-down economics sees societies' middle and lower classes gradually become more cash-strapped, fewer new businesses are created—and eventually we have the economic reality we have today, where millions of people on low incomes have their income subsidized by the government via things like food stamps and rental subsidies.

In a healthy economy, small businesses and enterprises typically contribute more than 50% of the overall gross domestic product of any country. Western governments, as a rule, should therefore make it easier for SMEs to establish themselves and flourish. Instead, the biggest economies allow big banks, private landlords, and investment funds to buy up all commercial real estate, which prevents new startups from ever being able to be anything but digital. Worse, when an economic storm hits, SMEs are usually thrown under the bus, while major banks and big industry players are thrown economic lifeline after economic lifeline—usually at the expense of taxpayers. This never used to be the way, though.

From 1250 until 1971, we had a perfect kind of money. We had representative money—an idea brought all the way from China by Marco Polo—which served us well for over 700 years because it mirrored exactly how true capitalism works.

As soon as we decoupled from representative money and the gold standard completely in 1971—at a time when the top taxpayers in America paid 90% tax and didn't really mind because they were so fabulously wealthy anyway—we saw deindustrialization start.

It was suddenly cheaper to import iron and steel from China. Then it was suddenly possible to manufacture everything the West might ever need in China.

At the same time, Ronald Reagan—a prominent proponent of trickle-down economics—began slashing top tax brackets from 90% to 50% to appease unions and industry in America. But unions and industry saw expected trickle-down dollars just trickle instead to China and other countries in Asia, where it was cheaper for corporations and brands to manufacture everything from branded apparel to the latest electronics.

The general public didn't find this alarming at the time, as they were learning to live off this fun new thing called credit—which is all you really have in a society that doesn't produce anything meaningful anymore, but which once used to and which still has a few big banks hanging around like vultures, hungry for the last morsels of wealth still available.

In truth, the only net benefit to America between 1980 and the year 2000—as the documentary filmmaker Michael Moore once put it simply—was a 305% increase in the number of people taking antidepressants.

It's Time to Reverse the Greatest Financial Coup d'État of the 20th Century

The answer to the next financial crisis, as far as 98% of world governments are concerned, is the implementation of Central Bank

Digital Currencies. I may be wrong when it comes to how this financial crisis manifests. Make no mistake, though: CBDCs are the planned solution.

Central Bank Digital Currencies will also be used benevolently in the beginning. They will probably even be celebrated. However, there will always be an eventual excuse—like a pandemic, war, or new economic threat—that sees banks and governments wield them more authoritatively. Once CBDCs are implemented, there is also no going back to the cash we have today.

In a fully implemented CBDC system, governments could financially exclude individuals or entire groups of people with the press of a button, leaving them with nothing. Governments like the CCP could target dissidents, sexual minorities, ethnic minorities, or religious minorities. If banknotes don't exist and access to government-issued digital cash is revoked, then they are truly helpless.

— Alex Gladstein, Human Rights Foundation

What is most egregious about our current predicament is that nothing happening today is by accident. If Abraham Lincoln's National Banking Acts of 1863 and 1864 had never been dismantled, the U.S. government would have retained control over U.S. monetary policy and the issuance of currency. Instead, all such powers were surrendered to the Federal Reserve upon its creation in 1913.

Likely, the United States would have never left the gold standard—and neither would the rest of the world have followed suit. Deindustrialization, inflation, the accumulation of massive government debts, and countermeasures such as bailouts and bail-ins have all been part of what can best be described as a massive financial coup d'état on the Western economy. The instigators of this coup d'état now want to do away with physical cash completely. The only question is: Will you let them?

"We don't know who's using a $100 bill today, and we don't know who's using a 1,000-peso bill today.

The key difference with the CBDC is the central bank will have absolute control on the rules and regulations that will determine the use of that expression of central bank liability, and also we will have the technology to enforce that."

— Agustín Carstens, General Manager, Bank for International Settlements

The Time to Ride the Crypto Wave Is Over

Warren Buffett, the sixty-year face of Berkshire Hathaway and long-time critic of cryptocurrency, once famously stated that he wouldn't buy all the Bitcoin in the world for $25. His reasoning is simple. Buffett only believes in investing in assets long-term. As a rule, Buffett will also never invest in an asset or business which he doesn't fully understand.

As it stands, no one really understands Bitcoin.

When was Bitcoin created and by whom? Put simply, no one knows. Bitcoin, after all, didn't start with the mining of the genesis block in 2009. Neither did the Bitcoin story really begin with Satoshi Nakamoto first publishing the Bitcoin whitepaper a year earlier.

Satoshi Nakamoto appearing suddenly out of nowhere to start seeding the Bitcoin.org forum in 2008 might seem like the start of the Bitcoin story. However, as anyone versed in cryptography, decentralized computing, and the basic mechanics of blockchain technology can verify, creating the code which underpins how Bitcoin works likely took several months or years. Likely, Bitcoin was also created by a group of people with backgrounds in several disparate academic disciplines.

Who were these people? When were the first lines of the Bitcoin codebase really written? Why also did Satoshi Nakamoto go to such extreme lengths to obfuscate his identity, only to almost immediately transfer ownership of the Bitcoin.org forum and the maintenance of Bitcoin itself to people who were very easy to identify?

Career investors like Warren Buffett ask themselves these questions to offset risk when investing. When no answers are forthcoming, they don't invest. Neither should this be surprising. Even parents warn children not to accept sweets from strangers.

Between 2009 and 2020, smart money watched Bitcoin from the sidelines. It was, therefore, predominantly retail investors who invested in Bitcoin and other cryptocurrencies and who made up the most significant part of the early cryptocurrency market. These were people with no real investing or trading experience, often limited cash to spare, and usually poor investing discipline.

To demonstrate, retail investors are often FOMO investors. They are reluctant to part with whatever cash they have available to invest; however, they also have a fear of missing out (FOMO) on opportunities to make significant returns. This often sees FOMO investors buy digital currencies like Bitcoin just as they are reaching new all-time price highs. Then, when markets reverse and prices start to fall, the same investors panic sell. This sees them sell digital assets like Bitcoin for markedly less than they originally bought them for.

The result? Smarter investors buy up coins that are being panic sold cheaply, then hold these for longer—often for several years or more—until they even consider selling. Meanwhile, more retail investors enter the market, and more get shaken out as they too are spooked into panic selling.

The Early Cryptocurrency Market Was Powered by the Average American

Why retail investors are prone to FOMO and panic selling is simple. It is estimated that the average working American has a mere $500 to $2,000 put aside as savings to use as a buffer against financial emergencies.

If you are such an American with a maximum liquidity of $2,000, you are of course going to sell any crypto you invest in when prices fall by 10%, 25%, or 50% or more. After all, what happens if you have a medical emergency or lose your job? You can't wait and hope that the price of Bitcoin rebounds during the next bull run. You might need as much cash as you can get your hands on tomorrow.

Even Forbes in 2017 predicted that the majority of early Bitcoin investors with enough discipline to hold Bitcoin long-term would likely liquidate investments when/if Bitcoin ever reached $100,000 to $127,000 in value. Why? Because this was the approximate amount of total debt held by most American households in 2017. If you are a young American and you suddenly have the opportunity to pay off all your debts with something you invested just a few hundred dollars in a few years ago, you would be stupid not to liquidate at $100,000.

Reaching almost $127,000 in value in November 2025, a Bitcoin selloff ensued just as Forbes predicted it might. Now, though, this selloff also represents something of a problem for Bitcoin.

If you were an average American with $1,000 and enough discipline to invest in Bitcoin long-term in 2015, you did so due to the belief that your $1,000 of Bitcoin might eventually be worth $100,000 or even $1 million in ten years' time. Fast forward to today, and even if Bitcoin reaches $1 million or $2 million by 2030 or 2035, investing $1,000 will only see you make a return of $10,000 or $20,000.

By comparison, investing in regular stocks like those of Amazon, Apple, or Tesla will see you likely make comparable or even greater returns, just with inherently less risk. Bitcoin, after all, is still just a speculative asset which only increases in value as more people buy the digital currency. When you buy it with a hope of making a mint in return, you are really buying it and hoping that other people do too.

Tech companies like Amazon, on the other hand, dominate actual cloud computing, e-commerce, and server markets.

Amazon stock in 2015 was valued at $33. Current prices stand at $229. That's a 1,300% price increase right there.

Put simply, the value of tech stocks increases as tech companies create in-demand products and services. By comparison, the value of cryptocurrency like Bitcoin is based solely on how much people have invested already, not future innovation.

The time to ride the Bitcoin wave is, if you like, over. This is at least the case if you are a retail investor. It simply doesn't make sense to put $1,000 or $2,000 in Bitcoin for the next decade when you can expect to make comparable or better returns investing in less speculative stocks which are also less volatile and which are traded on better-regulated markets.

At Present, 90% of New Cryptocurrency Investors Lose Everything

Lower returns for retail investors investing in Bitcoin since Bitcoin began trading for tens of thousands of dollars per coin has seen an explosion in meme coin trading and trading of so-called decentralized finance (DeFi) tokens. Sadly, the harsh reality of meme coin and DeFi trading and investing is that there is simply no substance to these markets.

Decentralized Finance (DeFi) is made to sound like a decentralized financial marketplace where participants in the DeFi ecosystem can purchase everything from the equivalent of home insurance, long-term savings bonds, and even decentralized mortgage products. In reality, nothing could be further from the truth.

In reality, DeFi marketplaces exist predominantly on Ethereum and emerging smart contract blockchains like Solana and Cardano. On these blockchains, people create decentralized cryptocurrency exchanges. These exchanges are then populated by people and groups who create new DeFi tokens or meme coins. Hype for such coins is then syndicated by X and other social media platforms. Investors who buy coins early often make 100% or 1,000% returns. However, these coins always drop abruptly in value to near zero within a matter of days, weeks, or sometimes even minutes. After they drop, they never recover. More coins simply enter the market to take their place. Investors who don't get out of the market quickly subsequently lose everything, just like most investors do in real-world Ponzi schemes.

Investing and trading meme coins is, if you like, essentially the same as hoping to get rich buying and trading penny stocks.

Legacy Cryptocurrencies Are Not the Future of Money

Bitcoin is often sold as an innovative decentralized, peer-to-peer, completely immutable digLegacy Cryptocurrencies Are Not the Future of Moneyital currency. Staunch proponents of Bitcoin like Max Keiser and Michael Saylor even suggest that Bitcoin and other legacy cryptocurrencies will one day become mainstream currencies used all around the world in everyday commerce. If not, they will become stores of value equivocal to precious metals like gold. In truth, though, this will never happen.

As I have made clear in The Crypto Con, Bitcoin is not peer-to-peer. If it was, you wouldn't pay a fee when transacting Bitcoin, and no middleman miner would be required to process a transaction for you. Neither is Bitcoin truly decentralized. Today, Bitcoin can best be described as partially decentralized, with most mining consolidated in

Asia. Bitcoin is also no longer immutable and is no longer anything of an innovation.

Every day, new cryptocurrency startups like Solana, Cardano, Zcash, etc., appear claiming that transactions on their blockchains process faster, are more private, are quantum computing resistant, etc. A more authentic description of Bitcoin should, therefore, read as:

Bitcoin was the world's first true blockchain-based digital currency, based on 2008 technologies in which all transactions are pseudo-anonymous.

Doesn't sound quite as catchy as a sales pitch, does it?

As for the 20,000+ other digital currencies which currently make up the global cryptocurrency market, none of them will ever be chosen to replace the cash or the digital equivalents of cash which we use at present.

As I hope I have made clear, global banks have already agreed that digital currency is a good thing. They even want the global economy to start shifting to an entirely cashless, cryptocurrency-centric future by as early as 2030. They just aren't going to use Chainlink, Bitcoin, Ethereum, Ripple XRP, or any other cryptocurrency currently on the market to do this.

Globally, central banks have been researching and developing their own proprietary cryptocurrencies for over a decade. To assume even for a second that there is any real chance that any legacy cryptocurrency you invest in might be the world's money of tomorrow is simply massively delusional.

Central Bank Digital Currencies will be created by banks, for banks, and be centrally managed by banks. Such banks will have no need of legacy cryptocurrencies like Bitcoin. Rather, it will be in such banks' interests to see legacy cryptocurrencies take leave of the financial scene completely.

Let's also be absolutely clear about what Bitcoin was in the beginning. Almost every new-to-market cryptocurrency investor today is entering the market simply because they want to get rich quickly by throwing a couple of hundred or thousand dollars at the right digital currency. However, this was never what Satoshi Nakamoto envisaged for cryptocurrency.

If Satoshi was real, it was clear from the beginning that his vision for Bitcoin was one in which the majority of people using Bitcoin would also be mining Bitcoin and helping maintain the Bitcoin network. Your computer would be your bank, and as you mined Bitcoin alongside millions of other individual miners, you would start spending and using Bitcoin in parallel with regular currencies, thereby planting the seeds of mainstream adoption as you did so.

It was Satoshi Nakamoto's plan for Bitcoin to slowly begin outshining existing fiat currency by gradually appreciating in value. Instead, it took less than three years for Bitcoin to become a mere get-rich-quick scheme where every year fewer individuals mine the currency. Now, the party is over. Even Michael Burry says so, and when Michael Burry says so, we know that the Bitcoin story—and perhaps the story of all cryptocurrency—is about to come full circle.

Who Is Michael Burry?

Central to the mythos of the Bitcoin origin story is the financial collapse of 2008. Bitcoin proponents cite the 2008 financial collapse as the very reason why Satoshi Nakamoto created Bitcoin in the first place. His reason for doing so? To help the world embrace a new kind of deflationary and decentralized digital currency which, if adopted, could unshackle humanity from the chains of monopolistic banks and inept governments and prevent anything like the same collapse from ever happening again. There is just one problem.

As anyone who is familiar with the movie The Big Short knows, the 2008 U.S. housing market collapse which instigated the greater 2008 global recession was forecast long in advance by the American investor and hedge fund manager Michael Burry. Burry being the character portrayed in The Big Short by the actor Christian Bale.

Despite being a Wall Street outsider and a medical doctor by training, the real-life Michael Burry saved his investor clients millions of dollars by steering clear of tech- and Internet-based stocks just before the bursting of the dot-com bubble at the turn of the millennium. Burry also spotted irregularities with the U.S. sub-prime mortgage market way back in 2003, five years before the eventual collapse of the U.S. housing market in 2008.

Fast forward to the present, and from as early as 2021, the very same Michael Burry has called out investing in Bitcoin as nothing more than Tulip Bulb Mania. This being a reference to the first speculative asset bubble in history, when between 1634 and 1637, Dutch tulip bulbs rose exponentially in value before demand suddenly plummeted and people realized that tulip bulbs really were just tulip bulbs.

As well as referring to Bitcoin as the Tulip Bulb bubble of our times, Michael Burry has more recently called out Bitcoin prices of $100,000 as absurd and "the most ridiculous thing" he has ever seen.

The irony here is nothing short of brutal. Bitcoin is often posited as a technologically innovative hedge against financial uncertainty. However, one of the world's respected authorities when it comes to spotting market downturns before they happen says that Bitcoin itself is nothing more than an absurd bubble. The only question is, when exactly will the Bitcoin bubble burst?

RIP Cryptocurrency - The Final Nail in the Coffin

In November 2025, something strange happened all across the 6 and a half million square mile territory of the Russian Federation.

In a matter of mere hours, every Porsche vehicle manufactured after 2013 was rendered completely immobile. Someone, somewhere, had seemingly activated a remote Porsche kill switch, and had likely done so via satellite. Many affected vehicles, after all, weren't in range of WiFi or cellular networks.

Later it was confirmed that a little-known feature called "The Porsche Vehicle Tracking System" was responsible. This being a discreet feature which uses satellite tracking to remotely deactivate engines of Porsche vehicles reported as stolen.

Russia was loath to admit that foreign government agencies like the CIA might be responsible for the Porsche Vehicle Tracking System failure. This, after all, would show weakness. However, in documents released by WikiLeaks in 2017, the ability to remotely deactivate individual vehicles and whole fleets of vehicles anywhere in the world is listed as a very real capability of the U.S. Central Intelligence Agency.

In a batch of leaks known as Vault 7, first leaked to WikiLeaks in 2016, it is also made clear that the CIA and NSA had, up until at least 2016, backdoor exploits into all Windows, Mac, and Linux computer operating systems, all smartphones, and all market-leading web browsers.

That such proven exploits exist is a clear, credible, and immediate threat to every form of cryptocurrency currently on the market.

If you store any crypto on your phone, it can be stolen. If you store any crypto you own on your computer, it can be stolen. If you use web browser–based apps like MetaMask to store and manage your cryptocurrency portfolio, your portfolio can be compromised. Such clandestine backdoors also allow agencies like the NSA and CIA to create massive botnets which could easily disrupt the real-time processing of transactions on blockchains like the Bitcoin blockchain.

Thanks to the leaks which make up Vault 7, we also know that up until at least 2016, U.S. intelligence agencies were utilizing such botnets to stage global cyber-attacks out of the U.S. embassy in Frankfurt, Germany. (Porsche itself, incidentally, is also based in Germany.) Often, U.S. intelligence services would also repurpose hacking tools stolen from rival agencies in Russia, North Korea, and Israel to make attacks look like the work of third-party foreign governments.

In such a cybersecurity landscape, the very idea that any kind of cryptocurrency has any kind of long-term viability is pathologically absurd.

Believe what you want. Believe that Satoshi Nakamoto was real and the most altruistic person in the world. It doesn't matter. His invention still remains vulnerable to a host of hardware- and software-based cybersecurity threats. Moreover, what we know of such threats today is likely just the tip of a massive global privacy-shattering iceberg.

Cryptocurrency Is Constantly Rebranding Itself

If you store gold or cash somewhere secret and secure, no one can take it from you. (At least not unless they utilize brute force.) By comparison, you could have anything from $5 to $5 million in cryptocurrency stored on your phone, computer, or an ultra-secure hardware wallet, only to wake up one day to find just digital dust where your balance used to be.

Remember that pesky Intel Management Engine with its own dedicated WiFi and Bluetooth networking capabilities? As of 2014, it is now possible for satellites orbiting 600 km above us to connect and interact with regular terrestrial Bluetooth chips, even if you can't connect to the likes of a Bluetooth speaker just a few meters away. However, it is not just increasing numbers of increasingly sophisticated cybersecurity threats which should deter people from investing in cryptocurrency.

Bitcoin was meant to work as a decentralized alternative to cash with transaction speeds comparable to Visa and Mastercard. Then the Bitcoin community decided that Bitcoin should instead serve as a store of wealth akin to so-called digital gold. Other coins like Litecoin and Dash, which could transact near-instantly, were then touted as the digital currencies which people should use in place of Bitcoin in everyday transactions.

July 2015 then saw the launch of Ethereum. Now the world had a digital currency which was also a decentralized virtual computer upon which everything from property to precious metals could be tokenized and traded. Try today, though, to exchange any tokenized gold you own on Ethereum for an equivalent amount of real-world gold you can hold in your hand and guess what—you can't.

Ethereum then rebranded itself as a platform upon which real-world startup businesses could raise capital necessary to launch via means of Initial Coin Offerings (ICOs).

Startups created coins which crypto investors could buy like regular shares in businesses. The idea was that as such businesses started trading profitably, ICO coin prices would increase or be redeemable against a percentage of such profits. To date, though, 61% of such ICO startups have failed to ever make returns for investors. In fact, only 1.5% of ICOs ever see investors make returns of 100% or more. Returns for the remaining 37.5% of ICO investors are usually in the 0.01% range.

Recent years have subsequently seen Ethereum steer away from ICOs to quietly rebrand itself as the No. 1 platform for trading non-fungible tokens. Bizarrely, such tokens predominantly took the form of unique caricatures of cats. When people began to realize that they were literally just buying cartoon images of cats which anyone could screenshot and use themselves, Ethereum then quietly rebranded once more to become the world's go-to platform for decentralized financial services. There is just one problem.

Regular financial services take the form of mortgage, loan, and insurance products. By comparison, the reality of most decentralized finance (DeFi) products is that they are just scams where every day, hundreds of new people create new tokens which rise exponentially in value as they hit DeFi exchanges, only to drop to near zero in a matter of days, weeks, or mere minutes afterward. Then they never recover. New tokens are simply created to take their place. Put simply, if you invest but don't get out of the market quickly enough, you lose everything.

To demonstrate, DeFi investors in 2023 lost a whopping $1.95 billion. Worse, investors in DeFi in April 2025 alone realized losses of over $92 million.

Bitcoin and Cryptocurrency Today Is Redundant in Real-Life Commerce

When Bitcoin first entered the spotlight of the mainstream media in late 2010, there were quiet rumbles of excitement. Major online freelance marketplaces like Fiverr and brands like Expedia were just some brands which by 2014 were happily accepting Bitcoin payments. Then, almost overnight, there wasn't just Bitcoin anymore. Instead, there were over 2,000 digital currencies on the market. Now today, there are over 20,000 and counting.

Logically, no business in the world is ever going to set up the payments infrastructure necessary to accommodate over 20,000 different digital currencies. Fees in Bitcoin today for simply buying a cup of coffee are often also greater than the cost of a cup of coffee itself. This is why the majority of businesses which accept cryptocurrency payments today do so via third-party payment processors.

Third-party payment processors take cryptocurrency intended for payment of goods and services, then exchange cryptocurrency for an equivalent amount of cash which businesses receive in lieu of actual Bitcoin or other digital currencies. This negates the risk to businesses of coins like Bitcoin suddenly plummeting in value and streamlines basic bookkeeping. However, this also means that cryptocurrency today has no real value in terms of it being used in regular commerce.

I Want to Believe & You Do Too

Was Bitcoin created by a three-letter agency like the NSA? At this point, it doesn't matter. The simple fact is that such agencies have the tools necessary to obliterate the cryptocurrency market overnight if they want to. It would also be folly to assume that the intelligence services of China and Russia don't also have the same capability. From a cybersecurity perspective, Bitcoin and every other legacy cryptocurrency on the market can be compromised.

If you are invested in cryptocurrency, you might not want to acknowledge this reality. Make no mistake, though; this is the reality we live in.

Is it true that the stablecoin Tether is just a ticking time bomb which will eventually wipe billions, possibly trillions, from the current cryptocurrency market? That ball is in Tether's court. A full independent audit of their accounts would settle the matter. All we know in the meantime is that Tether has previously lied about having enough liquid reserves to cover the billions of Tether coins in circulation and the billions more which it creates each and every month.

Is Donald Trump's Genius Act just a way to usher in Central Bank Digital Currencies by the back door? It doesn't matter. Regardless of how they arrive, CBDCs are the global banking establishment's planned replacement for regular bank currencies. It is also highly doubtful that legacy cryptocurrencies will be able to exist in tandem with this new monetary paradigm.

Is Bitcoin and are most other legacy cryptocurrencies completely worthless as a basic means of commercial exchange? Figure it out for yourself. Try using cryptocurrency to pay your rent and household bills for a month without first exchanging it (or having a third party exchange your crypto) for regular cash. Bitcoin is almost 20 years old and, well, mass adoption simply didn't happen.

Make no mistake. I didn't write The Crypto Con because I'm bitter about missing the train and not cramming as much Bitcoin as I could mine into a USB stick back in 2009.

I want the premise of Bitcoin to be real. I want Bitcoin to be truly, globally decentralized. I want every cryptocurrency transaction to be immutable. I want a deflationary form of currency I can use as a hedge against inflation and feel 100% comfortable pouring my pension into. This just isn't where the story of cryptocurrency has taken us, and that's probably our fault.

It might be that Satoshi Nakamoto was real and did have a virtuous ambition to free humanity from debt slavery and the unquenchable greed of governments, major banks and major corporations. Perhaps all he didn't factor into his equations was the fact that we're all inherently just as greedy, and that as such, Bitcoin was always going to come to parallel the existing machinations of the financial status quo we started with.

What Do We Do Now?

In The Crypto Con, I haven't merely attempted to reveal a certain level of incongruity surrounding the official Bitcoin origin story. Nor have I simply tried to shine a spotlight of acknowledgment on the very real threats to all cryptocurrencies posed by an ever-increasing number of ever-more-ingenious methods of electronic surveillance by international intelligence services.

In addition to all of the above, I have attempted to make readers aware of the very real and rapidly approaching danger posed by Central Bank Digital Currencies (CBDCs).

These are coming. If they are ever fully implemented, there will also be no going back to many of the basic personal and financial freedoms we take for granted today. The future I've attempted to help readers envisage with regard to CBDCs must, therefore, be resisted. There are also simple things people can do right now to demonstrate resistance.

Owning physical gold, as opposed to owning gold through indirect financial instruments has, from time immemorial, been the best way to safeguard personal wealth. Investing in and using local community banks, building societies, and credit unions also helps wrest control away from mainstream banks, many of which have been knowingly, yet discreetly, nudging customers toward a cashless future since at least 2008.

While they are convenient, ditching apps like Google Pay, Apple Pay, Revolut, Wise, and all their contemporaries in favor of using cash will also help keep demand for physical legal tender alive — as long as a significant percentage of the global population does the same.

As for how to make a fast fortune by investing: you can pump whatever you have into Bitcoin and other legacy cryptocurrencies if you really want. Just make sure to jump in a time machine and invest in 2009 like you should have done the first time.

www.ingramcontent.com/pod-product-compliance
Lightning Source LLC
LaVergne TN
LVHW100311210926
848480LV00003B/1092
* 9 7 9 8 2 3 3 1 4 0 3 1 0 *